PRAISE FOR TOM STONE

"Tom Stone has done something quite unique. He has distilled out of his vast experience the simplest and most useful tools for creating profound and lasting change in our lives. I am truly grateful to Tom for his help in my own life and I am delighted that he is sharing his insights and techniques to help others on a large scale. I know his desire is very similar to mine—to have a positive impact on the lives of many, many people. I know that through his pioneering work in **Human Software Engineering** he will accomplish this goal in a profound and powerful way."

—Jack Canfield, *Chicken Soup for the Soul®*

"Tom Stone is nothing short of a genius. He is an expert in the area of dynamics, and he has the cleanest energy of ANYONE I've ever met, bar none. Even good coaches make an average of 20 coaching mistakes per session, but when I met with Tom, he made only one mistake—and then he immediately caught himself and corrected it! I was really amazed, and I immediately asked him to be my personal coach. I guess that makes him the coach to the coach to the coaches!"

—Thomas Leonard, Founder of *CoachVille* and Life Coaching Industry Pioneer

PRAISE FOR PURE AWARENESS

"The *Pure Awareness* Techniques that Tom Stone shares in this book have had a profound effect on my life. I became involved in the field of energy psychology early on and I believe that these methods can be used by every therapist, counselor, addiction specialist, life coach, and anyone who is interested in improving their life. I think you will be amazed and delighted at how rapid and simple these transformational tools are to practice."

—George J. Pratt, Ph.D., Chairman,
Psychology, Scripps Memorial Hospital, La Jolla,
Coauthor, *Instant Emotional Healing:
Accupressure for the Emotions*

"I've used these techniques on a daily basis and continue to do so. As a result, today I experience a sense of continuous inner peace and connection with my Self."

—Colleen Moore, Licensed Marriage
and Family Therapist, Auburn, CA

PRAISE FOR CORE DYNAMICS COACHING™

"After attending the *Core Dynamics* training in Phoenix, I threw away every other coaching strategy and tool I've ever learned because I don't need them anymore. People are coming from all over for appointments and are reporting transformations of mind-blowing proportions. There is no way to overstate the importance of the *Core Dynamics* training for coaching."

—Wendy Down, Master Certified Coach,
Brantford, Ontario

"We may have come to some wrong conclusions in the past and the *Core Dynamics* method showed me how I could update my perspective to be more successful and effective both in business and in life. We often think that logic and intellect should be the only driver for business, but in the *Core Dynamics* Coach Training, I was shown how much power is available to us when we use all of who we are, including our emotions."

—Val Williams, Master Certified Coach,
Metuchen, NJA

ABOUT THE AUTHOR

Tom Stone is an internationally acclaimed speaker and seminar presenter, as well as an inventor, writer and entrepreneur. He has spent much of his life developing the most efficient and effective techniques for solving problems using principles and techniques from biophysics.

Tom is the pioneer of the new emerging field of **Human Software Engineering**™ (HSE) in which he has made a number of unique discoveries, including a set of profound insights into the nature of human conditioning, which he calls the CORE DYNAMICS OF HUMAN CONDITIONING.™ This unique body of work provides the tools for easily eliminating the barriers and blocks that weigh people down, infringe on potential, and keep people from having the life they truly want.

Tom has turned his focus in recent years to finding effective, non-medicinal solutions to many of the seemingly intractable problems that plague modern society, such as anxiety, depression, PTSD, and ADD/ADHD. This book is the culmination of several years of intensive research and is the first in the *Vaporize Your Problems* series. Tom lives in Carlsbad, California and is founder and CEO Great Life Technologies where he directs the Great Life Coaching Center.

Please visit www.vaporizeyouranxiety.com to learn more about Tom's work.

Vaporize your ANXIETY

without drugs or therapy

TOM STONE

Vaporize Your Anxiety

Published by:
Great Life Technologies, Inc.
2385 Camino Vida Roble, Suite 204
Carlsbad, CA 92011
(888) 928-3625
www.greatlifetechnologies.com

ISBN: 978-0-9825391-0-1

*This book is dedicated
to everyone who would
like to be free from
anxiety.*

Acknowledgments

I am most grateful to my wife Lynda who has always supported me wholeheartedly in my work and creative projects, especially the writing of this and my other books.

I am deeply grateful to Michael Stratford for his contribution to the special application of the GAP technique called SANYAMA and his delightful collaboration in co-creating and teaching the *Core Dynamics* Coach Training Program with me.

Thanks to David Jakoby, Aimee Snow and Cathi Stevenson for their contributions to the first edition of this book.

I am particularly grateful to all of my clients, seminar and training program participants, the *Core Dynamics* Coaches and Teachers, the WaveMaker Coaches and Human Software Engineers who have so whole-heartedly embraced this work and who have provided an environment in which these techniques could be refined and perfected over the years. It is these pioneers of **Human Software Engineering** who are really propagating this work in the world. To all of you I offer my heartfelt thanks.

I am especially grateful to Antoinette Kuritz of Strategies Literary and Public Relations for her superb guidance and editing of this second edition of *Vaporize Your Anxiety without Drugs or Therapy* as well as the excellent public relations campaign she crafted for the promotion of this book. I am blessed to have such a terrific collaborator.

Special thanks to Gwyn Kennedy Snider of GKS Creative for the terrific job on the cover and layout of the book.

And I am grateful to you dear reader for having the courage to open these pages and explore new solutions to the age-old problem of anxiety. May you use and enjoy the precious techniques presented here and may they help you to *Vaporize Your Anxiety* for the rest of your life!

Tom Stone
Carlsbad, California
April 2010

Contents

x

HOW TO USE THIS BOOK

One of the most common illnesses in the U.S., anxiety disorders, affects 40 million adults ages 18 and older, or 18.1 percent of the U.S. population. You cannot turn on the TV or read a magazine without seeing an ad for anti-anxiety medication, the ads even suggesting that you bring the medication and your need for it to the attention of your physician.

While there is no doubt that in some cases medication is indicated, medication is at best a symptom suppressive coping mechanism, not a cure. And for most of us anxiety can be managed or even eradicated without the use of drugs or traditional therapy. That's what this book is about. It is a road map to taking the reins of your anxiety and literally vaporizing it.

As a practitioner and teacher of Transcendental Meditation for over 30 years, I found that as effective as it was for experiencing consciousness and relieving stress, when it came to anxiety and other emotional challenges, something even more was needed. Even after 30 years of meditation, I would find myself caught in the grip of emotional reactions for days or even weeks at a time. And I wasn't alone. I noticed that this was true for many of my long-term meditator friends, too.

While the techniques that you will learn in this book are somewhat similar to meditation, there are crucial differences that make these techniques highly effective for resolving anxiety in a fraction of the time that it would take with even the most effective meditation techniques.

Regardless of your level of experience with meditation, the exercises and techniques taught in this book will be easy to implement. If you are already familiar with meditation, you will enjoy the unique and powerful differences between meditation and the techniques taught herein. If you have never practiced meditation, you will find the GAP Technique to be the simplest and quickest way to gain the experience of what is called *Pure Awareness*, a state in which anxiety simply doesn't exist.

Anxiety is often an emotional reaction to unhealed emotional traumas. This book is the culmination of many years of research to discover the nature of what causes us to stay stuck in the emotional reactions that prevent self-healing from old emotional traumas. Most meditation techniques are designed to control the mind, contemplate something laudable or, with the best forms of meditation, provide the experience of your *essential nature*, your own consciousness. Some of the *Pure Awareness* Techniques in this book also guide you to this kind of experience. But others take it quite a bit further. What's missing with traditional meditation techniques are effective and efficient ways to resolve emotional reactivity and traumas. These are the real barriers to attaining a stable state of higher consciousness, and they are the very things that are at the root of problems like anxiety.

Having already taken the journey upon which you are embarking, I look forward to sharing with you these liberating tools and techniques that will free you from the grip of anxiety and open up a whole new world in which you hold the reins of your emotional well-being.

GLOSSARY

I'll be using some terms like *Pure Awareness*, the *Core Dynamics* of Human Conditioning and other expressions that I want to clarify for you up front. I want you to be clear about what I mean by these terms so that there are no obstacles to your getting the real value out of the concepts and techniques that I am presenting here. The following is a glossary of the terms you will encounter as you *Vaporize Your Anxiety*. I'll give you enough to get you started here and explain these ideas in greater detail throughout the book.

OK, here we go –

ANXIETY – Although there may be many definitions of anxiety, *in this book we consider anxiety to be the experience of dancing around the outer edges of fear.* Anxiety is not a separate experience from fear. It is the lightweight version of fear. It is a conditioned reaction to move away from where the energy of fear is the most intense so that it doesn't overwhelm us. What we need are new techniques for quickly and completely resolving the underlying fear at the basis of the experience that we call anxiety.

CORE DYNAMICS – This is the abbreviated expression for the longer term—***The Core Dynamics of Human Conditioning***. It is a set of 12 penetrating insights into the nature of preverbal conditioning. As you'll see, it provides a kind of road map of the nature of our highly limiting, very early, *feeling-level decisions* that then impact us throughout our lives, usually without our even being aware that they are there. **The Core Dynamics** can also be thought of as *illusions of separateness*, the patterns of conditioning that prevent us from being clear about who and what we really are. *Put simply,* **The Core Dynamics** *are our often sub-conscious core reasons for acting, reacting, and responding the way we do to certain stimuli.*

PURE AWARENESS TECHNIQUES – *This is a set of breakthrough, experiential techniques that you will learn throughout the book that can help you to* **Vaporize Your Anxiety**. They are very likely quite different than anything you have experienced before. They guide you to have experiences that are the opposite of what you have been deeply conditioned to do by the presence of the conditioning of the *Core Dynamics*. They guide you to *Pure Awareness,* a state of optimal integrated reality.

THE SEE TECHNIQUE – This is the acronym for one of the *Pure Awareness Techniques*. We all have heard the expression about not being able to see the forest for the trees. Between anxiety and the conditioning of the *Core Dynamics*, this is often the case. *The SEE Technique*, standing for *Side Entrance Expansion*, is a unique method of taking your awareness out past the outer edge of the energy field of an emotional reaction. Once you get past the outer edge of the energy field of your emotion (which is quite easy to do) the emotion simply fades away and is gone. You'll be amazed at how quickly and effectively this resolves anxiety. *Put simply, The SEE Technique brings you past reactionary emotion so that you can Vaporize Your Anxiety.*

THE CORE TECHNIQUE – Another of the *Pure Awareness Techniques*, this one guides you into the center of the intensity of the energy field of incomplete emotional traumas, traumas which you were previously unable to resolve. Although that doesn't sound like much fun, it is actually much easier than you think. It is only the conditioned fear of being overwhelmed, held by the three-year old inside of us, that is terrified by the prospect of this. Once you get the hang of it, it's a piece of cake to resolve even the most intense, incomplete emotional pain that is often the underpinning of our anxiety. *With the CORE Technique, you will be resolving any traumatic underpinnings that may be at the basis of your anxiety.*

PURE AWARENESS – *Pure Awareness* means the experience of awareness itself without the distraction of being aware of some object of experience. This is a unique experience as we are usually aware of some thing.

Pure Awareness is the stripping away of all the externals; it is the experience of awareness being aware of itself; it is the ultimate, naked self-knowledge.

THE GAP TECHNIQUE – **GAP** stands for *Greater Awareness Place* and it is a *Pure Awareness Technique* for directly experiencing your own awareness all by itself. Thus it is a direct and simple way to experience *Pure Awareness* described above. It is done by looking off to the side of your thoughts and noticing that the thoughts are occurring in a background of silence. That silence is your own awareness.

THE GPS TECHNIQUE – **GPS** stands for *Gentle Provocation System* and is a *Pure Awareness Technique* for gently gaining access to the experience of the energy of an emotion held in the body, particularly when access doesn't seem possible by thinking or talking about an issue. The GPS Technique takes you into a heightened level of Self-Awareness that helps you to clear away the debris of unresolved issues. I consider it to be like a vacuum cleaner of energy patterns of emotional *dust-bunnies*.

THE SANYAMA TECHNIQUE™ – *Silent Awareness Notices Your Answers Manifesting Automatically*. Need a better understanding of something? Need to settle an internal issue? This *Pure Awareness Technique* starts with the *GAP*, experiencing *Pure Awareness,* and then dropping an inquiry into *Pure Awareness*. It is a way of getting clarity about something and is also the basis of the *GPS Technique.*

WHOLENESS – Problems in human life are caused by the loss of the experience of **Wholeness**. *In this context wholeness means experiencing yourself as whole and complete.* This is the experience that you have when you are in **Pure Awareness**. We lose the experience of **Wholeness** when we are absorbed in the *illusions of separateness* of the **Core Dynamics**, when we become the sum of the impact of our conditioning.

THE ACE STUDY – *The Adverse Childhood Experiences Study* is a massive scientific study done at Kaiser-Permanente in San Diego, California with over 17,000 Kaiser members. The study correlates the number of categories of childhood traumas to the occurrence of adult behavioral and physical health problems. This study quantifies what many of us intuitively know, that unresolved emotional traumas are the basis of a great many health problems.

GATEKEEPER – This is a special case of having an emotional energy present inside of you that prevents you from resolving yet other emotions. Like a guard standing in front of a castle door, it won't let you in to fully resolve an emotion. This is because the emotion has been with you so long that it feels like it is actually a part of you. It is part of your self-definition. And the *Gatekeeper* is the fear that if you let go of that emotion, you will lose part of yourself. You won't know who you are anymore. *Gatekeepers are parasitic emotional energy that we mistakenly assume as part of our integral selves and by which we, in part, define ourselves.* They are very commonly present with long-term anxiety and have to be resolved before the fear that is creating the anxiety itself can be fully resolved.

TOOLS AND TECHNIQUES

This book will provide you with tools and techniques you can start using *today* that will liberate you from the grip of anxiety without the use of drugs or traditional therapy. But to use them, you will have to be committed and open-minded.

My experience guiding many hundreds of people with these techniques has demonstrated that relief from anxiety and worry can occur within minutes of learning and using them. Although they are probably very different from anything you've experienced before, they are quite easy to learn and apply. And as you'll see, once you begin practicing them, a whole new world will open up to you, allowing you to experience more joy, fulfillment, and success than you ever thought possible.

We have all met people who seem defined by their problems, by their drama, who seem to equate suffering with purpose. But no one is happy in this paradigm. And it is merely an exaggeration of the condition in which many of us do exist.

When powerful emotional problems are literally vaporized, it becomes possible, perhaps for the first time in your life, to step away from your suffering. This is a seminal experience because many of us are so completely identified *with* our suffering. When you're free of it, you become present for life's greatest gift:

the true experience of who and what you really are. You'll suddenly find that you won't spend time *questioning* who you are any more, so much as *experiencing* who you are. You'll find that you have access to the one thing that makes true happiness and productivity possible. It's the thing we're all after, and it's the one thing that for many of us seems so out of reach: *Peace of Mind.*

These are big promises, and I need to emphasize that just reading this book will not free you from worry and anxiety. You'll need to put the techniques into *practice* and you'll need to *remember to use them.* But when you do, you'll find that you've gone beyond putting a band-aid on your anxiety. You will have actually *resolved* the problems at their core, so if anxiety rears its ugly head again you'll know just how to resolve it quickly and thoroughly. What I've found time after time is that anyone can be freed from anxiety when they use these tools consistently and diligently.

Part I of *Vaporize Your Anxiety* is a discussion of the various theories and research that form the foundation of the techniques we use. Those of you who have not had any familiarity with my work should be sure to read this section. I cover all the relevant information you'll need in order to understand how you're going to proceed. If you are familiar with my work, this chapter will serve as a refresher.

Part II of the book is a practical guide, providing you with exercises and instructions so you can begin to *Vaporize Your Anxiety* right away.

You are embarking on a journey at the end of which you will feel more alive, more attuned, more in touch with and appreciative of your *SELF*. It is an adventure that will take you to ***Pure Awareness*** and peace of mind. Enjoy.

To Your Health and Well-being,
Tom Stone
April 2010

Vaporize
your
ANXIETY

PART I
The Problem

CHAPTER 1

Facing the Challenge of Anxiety

THE SCOPE OF THE PROBLEM

If you suffer from anxiety, you are not alone. According to the Anxiety Disorders Association of America (ADAA), an estimated 40 million Americans over the age of 18 suffer from an anxiety disorder.[1] Anxiety disorders are therefore the most common mental illness in the U.S., with over 18% of the adult U.S. population (age 18 and older) affected. That means that one in seven people in the U.S. are struggling with anxiety on an ongoing basis. Further, approximately one-third of American adults will have at least one anxiety or panic attack in their lifetimes. This startling data reveals that anxiety is the most prevalent emotional disorder in the U.S.—more common even than alcohol abuse or depression.

According to "The Economic Burden of Anxiety Disorders," a study commissioned by the ADAA and based

1 http://www.adaa.org/AboutADAA/PressRoom/Stats&Facts.asp

on data gathered by the association and published in the Journal of Clinical Psychiatry, anxiety disorders cost the U.S. more than $42 billion a year—almost one third of the $148 billion total mental health bill for the U.S. More than $22.84 billion of those costs are associated with the repeated use of healthcare services, as those with anxiety disorders seek relief for symptoms that mimic physical illnesses. Indeed, people with an anxiety disorder are three-to-five times more likely to go to the doctor and six times more likely to be hospitalized for psychiatric disorders than non-sufferers.[2]

These figures make it clear that we are in the midst of a mental health crisis. Worse, for all our supposed medical sophistication, we don't even seem to be making a dent in the problem. We self-medicate, we seek therapists, and yet we stay anxious. What can be done?

WHAT IS ANXIETY, REALLY?

In dealing with anxiety, as in dealing with most mental health disorders, two protocols are the norm: counseling to get to the root of the problem and medication to help deal with the effects of the disorder. This approach is often long-term and expensive with the medication itself causing unwanted side-effects.

> Anxiety is dancing around the outer edges of fear.

2   ibid

While there are many theories about anxiety and how to deal with it, I take a very simple approach based on practical, experiential wisdom. Although this book endeavors to offer penetrating and valuable insights into why humans tend to develop anxiety, my true focus is on offering techniques that will help to rapidly and thoroughly resolve this widespread problem without the use of drugs.

Our approach looks beyond a strictly biochemical or genetic point of view and considers instead that the experience of anxiety occurs as the result of being stuck at the outer edge of fear—afraid, in a sense, of the deeper, overwhelming energy of fear—without proper tools or training to resolve it. When this happens, fear continues to be held in the body without resolution. Anxiety is simply our attempt to avoid being overwhelmed by fear; it keeps us from having to face the true epicenter of our emotion. This "coping strategy" (that is, trying to avoid being overwhelmed by the energy of the fear) is the best we can do, so we stay stuck in an eternal, anxious dance around the outer edges of fear.

> Anxiety is simply our body's attempt to avoid being overwhelmed by fear

The reason we reach this state is that we haven't learned to effectively resolve intense emotional reactions and traumas. Our early childhood conditioning compounds the problem, and while not everyone experiences problems with anxiety, this underlying conditioning does appear to be pretty universal. And as you will see from reading Chapter 4 on the ACE Study, the severity of the conditioning can determine why some people have problems with anxiety and others don't.

HUMAN SOFTWARE ENGINEERING

The insights and techniques taught in this book were developed as a part of an emerging field called **Human Software Engineering**, which is based on the idea that humans are a lot like computers. After all, we created computers to automate certain human tasks, so it makes sense that in many ways, they behave like we do. And as computers become more sophisticated, they become more and more like us. What is interesting is that we can learn some very useful things about ourselves by thinking about how computers work. As it turns out, terms like *software*, *hardware*, *virus*, and *bugs* are all surprisingly effective for describing both what's going on with us, and how to improve it.

Computers are much less complex than we are. In fact, any researcher in the field of neuroscience will tell you that the human brain is infinitely more complex than the most complex computer on earth. And while we have the capacity to understand the most complex computers, we still are only scratching the surface of our understanding of the human brain.

A computer does two things: it receives requests and it responds to them. When you open up your email account and you hit *get new mail*, you're making a request to the computer, and the computer responds by putting all your new emails into your inbox. Obviously, it's a little more complicated than that, but in the simplest terms, *request then response* is all that's really ever happening in your computer, or even when you're using the Internet.

Now, when your computer has a bug, it's like a little glitch that prevents the computer from either responding at all, or from responding correctly. For example, you might double click on a document to try to open it, but if you don't have the software program the document was created with, your computer won't give you any response except maybe *"I can't give you a response,"* or *"Program Not Found."*

If you do have the program, but there happens to be a bug somewhere in the document or in your software program, you might open it up and see a bunch of gobbledygook. Have you ever opened up a web page or a document and seen a bunch of squares and slashes and circles? Your computer is giving you a response—it's just the wrong one.

Much like computers, humans have *bugs* too. For some people, these bugs cause procrastination or anger, or even addictive behaviors. And for many others, they cause anxiety and anxiety-related emotional problems. Think about this for a moment: scroll through your daily life and stop to think about your *problems*. If you're like most people, you probably have a handful of problems that keep coming up, over and over. Maybe it's having the nerve to speak your mind to superiors at work, or to your spouse. Maybe it's eating certain foods you know aren't good for you. Maybe it's something as simple as being lazy about flossing!

> Much like computers, humans have bugs, too. For some people, these bugs cause procrastination or anger, or even addictive behaviors. For many others, they cause anxiety and anxiety-related emotional problems.

If you think about it, you will realize that in each case, what's happening is that you're making a request—*"Could you please talk to your boss about how ridiculously low your salary is?"*—but you're getting either no response (*"Sorry, didn't hear you. I think I'll go get a cup of coffee and then go back to my desk"*), or you're getting the wrong response entirely (you go talk to your boss, but when you open your mouth, what comes out is something like *"I love your new suit! Oh, and by the way, I'm really enjoying that new project. Okay, see you later!"* And you walk dejectedly back to your desk.) You know what you want to do, but you cannot seem to accomplish it. These are your bugs affecting your responses and actions.

The tools in this book, as well as the exclusive audio recordings available at www.vaporizeyouranxiety.com, will teach you how to literally *debug* your *inner human software*, and in the process, quickly reduce and very likely eliminate your anxiety completely. As I said earlier, however, to have true success with these techniques, it is very important to learn them thoroughly and to remember to use them regularly. I can't emphasize this enough. Please read this book from start to finish, and take the time to stop and practice when indicated. Practice often, until the techniques become second nature. Once you start to get a feel for them, you'll find yourself doing them almost automatically whenever needed.

Audio recording of the techniques at:
www.vaporizeyouranxiety.com/resources.html

In this book, you're going to learn to do some things that are in many cases the exact opposite of what you've been deeply conditioned to do. But the truth is, even though they may seem strange and unfamiliar at first, they are really quite natural and anyone can easily learn to do them. And besides, if you have come to the realization that what you've been doing up until now hasn't gotten rid of your anxiety, it's safe to assume that something *really different* is *exactly* what you need.

There is one other thing I would like to mention here. If you've been experiencing anxiety for a long time, the idea that you can eliminate it quickly and completely might sound a bit unreal. In fact, because it sounds like such an outrageous claim, it might be enough to trigger anxiety about whether or not this could possibly be true. But so many people have been successful with vaporizing their anxiety using these techniques that I feel compelled to share these great breakthroughs with everyone who suffers unnecessarily from anxiety—and to reassure you that you will almost definitely experience results. I sincerely hope that you will apply these techniques consistently so that you too can *Vaporize Your Anxiety* and be free to live as you wish.

CHAPTER 2

The Set Up

HOW PREVERBAL CONDITIONING
SETS US UP TO BE ANXIOUS

Before we get into the actual techniques, I would like to take a moment to explain how they came about. **Human Software Engineering** and the techniques for vaporizing your anxiety are based on a set of profound insights into the nature of what is called *preverbal human conditioning*. These insights came after many years of research into what happens before we have words to describe our experiences.

> Anxiety is the result of decisions we made about life and about ourselves before we had words to describe them

As it turns out, anxiety, like many of the emotional problems that plague us in our adult lives, is the result of decisions about life and about ourselves that we made before we had words to describe them.

When we're very young—one, two, three years old—we don't yet have language. However, although we don't have words, we do have something else in great abundance: *feelings*! We may not have names for these feelings yet, but we *have* them and we live inside them every moment of every day.

As infants and toddlers, we are often confronted with situations that make us feel emotionally overwhelmed. Because there are so many of these situations we must face, and because the feeling of being emotionally overwhelmed is so uncomfortable, we end up making *feeling-level decisions—preverbal decisions*—to put a lid on accessing our own innate capacity to feel. The problem is that in our early life, we make a whole lot of these decisions about life and about ourselves.

> As we grow, our bodies and brains acquire more and more hardware for processing feelings. But because we've been conditioned to avoid intense emotional experiences, this increased capacity tends to be grossly underutilized.

This concept of how preverbal conditioning operates has been substantiated by extensive scientific research on emotions and the brain. Using the newest generation of brain-scanning devices, researchers have discovered cells in the brain that are directly responsible for processing emotional experiences. While being scanned, subjects were given emotional stimuli, and the brain cells that were activated were monitored. These cells—called *spindle cells*—experienced increased blood flow during the period of emotional stimulation. These findings leave little doubt that spindle cells are involved with the processing of emotional information[3].

There are *relatively few spindle cells in our brain during infancy*. So when we're still very young, we really don't have much capacity to feel and process our emotions. We just don't have the *physical hardware* to do it. But between infancy and adulthood, there is ap-

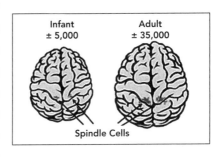

parently about a sevenfold increase in the number of spindle cells in the brain, and therefore a substantial increase in our capacity to experience a wider range of emotions. What this means is that as we grow, our bodies and brains acquire more and more *hardware* for processing feelings. But because we've been conditioned to avoid intense emotional experiences, this increased

---

3   Blakeslee, Sandra. "Humanity? Maybe It's in the Wiring." New York Times, December 9, 2003.

capacity tends to be grossly underutilized. The old notion that *humans only use ten percent of their brain capacity* has generally been debunked, but when it comes to our ability to feel, it looks like this may actually be pretty accurate!

As we grow, our bodies and brains acquire more and more *hardware* for processing feelings. But because we've been conditioned to avoid intense emotional experiences, this increased capacity tends to be grossly underutilized.

UNDERUTILIZATION OF OUR INNATE CAPACITY TOO FEEL

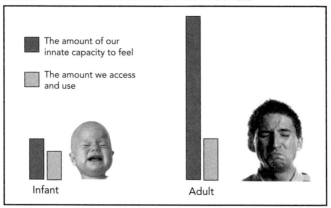

The amount of our innate capacity to feel

The amount we access and use

Infant

Adult

As infants and toddlers, we tend to act on feelings. And often, those actions meet with disapproval or manipulation, causing us to eventually abrogate our feelings. For example, it seems to be pretty universal that one day during your first years, you might get an inspiration to do something like paint a picture all over your bedroom wall with a felt-tip marker or attempt to put lipstick on the dog. It is not an action we take spitefully. As infants or toddlers we do these things spontaneously, creatively, and with joy. But what happens? Your parents find out, they express disapproval, and you get punished. All of a sudden, your source of supply for everything—love, food, and protection—turns on you. And what is it that you got punished for? Essentially, it was for acting in a very pure way, based on an inner impulse. You didn't think. You just felt inspiration and took action. But your parents are inadvertently playing a game that we might call - *Let's socialize the kids through emotional manipulation*. So now you make another of these feeling-level decisions. And this one is: *I'm not going to act on my creative intuition or with spontaneity, because when I do, I get cut off from the things I need in order to survive*. But of course you don't have this level of sophistication of language yet, if you have language at all. You have acted out of pureness, and that pureness has been attacked. You do not yet know 'right from wrong' and yet you are punished, you suffer disapproval. And it is in seeking to avoid the negativity that we begin to bury our natural enthusiasm, our natural responses.

So these preverbal feeling-level decisions become blocks that later keep you from experiencing your emotions fully. Because you get overwhelmed and then punished, it doesn't take many of these experiences for you to simply put a lid on allowing yourself access to your natural capacity to feel your feelings fully. As a result, you tend not to complete intense emotional experiences and they accumulate in your body. You end up with a kind of storehouse of incomplete emotional experiences archived inside of you.

And then, right as you were building up a stockpile of these incomplete emotional experiences, something very curious happens. At about the age of three or four, you begin to make an enormous shift, and you start relating to the world primarily through words. Where once you were *preverbal*, you are now *verbal*. And as a result, you forget that you made all these feeling-level decisions in the first place. You forget the whole stockpile of incomplete emotional experiences, but they are still there stored on the hard drive called your body. The incredible thing that research into **Human Software Engineering** has shown is that even though we didn't have words, we were still capable of making very real, lasting decisions about ourselves and about the world around us. And so, while they are now catalogued, those initial decisions are still with us and still have an impact.

When we *became verbal* we lost access to a real connection with the feeling-level world we lived in previously and in which we made all those important early decisions. We literally *crossed over into the world of words*, and lost our ability to change these decisions because they were non-verbal, and they just didn't respond to words. That's why anxiety—which is a direct result of these preverbal, feeling-level decisions, is typically so resistant to change using traditional therapy or self-help books. It's a little like trying to *see* music, or *touch* the smell of a cake baking. It's just the wrong set of tools.

So the problem we face as adults is that although we've forgotten them, these feeling-level decisions are still lodged in our consciousness at a very deep level, beyond what we can describe. And unfortunately, they tend to dictate everything we do. We live inside their incredibly limiting influence without even realizing it, cut off from the experience of who we really are.

> Anxiety itself is really nothing but the inability to fully experience the intense emotional energy of fear that is held in the body.

My research over the last 15 years has been focused primarily on discovering what the real bugs are that junk up our inner human software. What I've discovered is that for the most part, it's those same feeling-level decisions or preverbal conditioning. And it is this very kind of *preverbal, feeling-level decision* that is the real basis of anxiety. Anxiety itself is really nothing but the inability to fully experience the intense emotional energy of fear that is held in the body.

Of course, the question is, *"What can we do about it?"* To answer this, we need to talk a little bit about feelings, but in a different way than you may be used to.

JUST WHAT ARE FEELINGS, ANYWAY?

> All emotions are just patterns of energy created within us as a response to some stimulus.

One of the foundational principles of quantum mechanics is that everything is produced out of a field of pure potentiality, a limitless field of pure energy and information that has not yet become expressed in any physical form. The theory is that everything we experience is created from this field of pure potential. Everything, say the quantum physicists, is energy: the book you're holding in your hands, the bones in your body, the windshield on your car. And if everything is energy, this must also include our feelings.

This is not really so hard to understand. In fact, we know intuitively that our brains and bodies create the experience of emotion as a response to some outer stimulus. For example, when we feel physically threatened, we may respond with a *fight, flight, or freeze* response. These responses are natural to all living creatures. We all have basic survival instincts built into us. Even flies don't want to be swatted—so they fly away if they can.

What we need to recognize, however, is that *all* emotions are just patterns of energy we create within ourselves as an automatic response to a stimulus. Because different emotions have different vibrational patterns to them, we are able to distinguish between them. We then *label* them according to the particular sensation we experience.[4,5] Thus we say *fear, sadness, anger, anxiety, happiness, elation, and so forth.* This is because we inhabit the verbal world, and need some way to communicate our experiences with others. But contrary to common belief, feelings are not *mental experiences.* Granted, your mind may be running wild with all kinds of thoughts about the emotion: how to get rid of it, what caused it, how you're a victim of it, and so forth. But these are just thoughts or stories, conjured up to attempt to *explain* the experience of this energy in our body. They are not the emotion itself.

It is very important to grasp this concept, because as you'll see, the techniques you'll soon be using to *Vaporize Your Anxiety* are based on this way of seeing feelings as patterns of energy that we experience in our bodies.

---

4 Institute of HeartMath, a non-profit research organization that investigates emotional energy and intuitive development

5 Power vs. Force: The Hidden Determinants of Human Behavior, by David R. Hawkins, MD, PhD

CHAPTER 3

The ACE Study & The Inability to Self-Heal Emotional Pain

[
If risk factors for disease, disability, and early mortality are not randomly distributed, what influences precede the adoption or development of them?
]

In the summer of 2005, I read about a scientific study called the Adverse Childhood Experiences (ACE) Study, which was described in an article entitled "The Relation Between Adverse Childhood Experiences and Adult Health: Turning Gold into Lead," by Vincent J. Felitti, M.D.[6]

At the time, Dr. Felitti was head of the Department of Preventive Medicine at Kaiser Permanente in San Diego. His co-researcher for the study was Dr. Robert Anda of the Center for Disease Control. This major study, which involved 17,421 adult Kaiser Health Plan members, reveals a powerful relationship between, on the one hand, childhood emotional experiences, and on the other, adult physical and emotional health, major illness, and even early death.

THE ACE PYRAMID, SHOWING THE PROGRESSION FROM ADVERSE CHILDHOOD EXPERIENCES TO EARLY DEATH

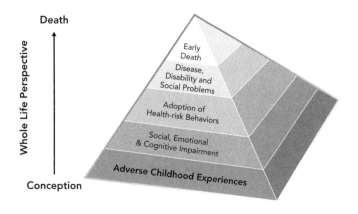

The ACE Pyramid represents the conceptual framework for the study. In the 1980s and early 1990s, information about risk factors for disease had been widely researched and merged into public education and prevention programs. It became clear that many risk factors—such as smoking, alcohol abuse, and sexual behaviors that put people at risk for certain diseases—were not randomly distributed in the population. In fact, it was known that risk factors for many chronic diseases tended to cluster—that is, persons who had one risk factor tended to have one or more others. The ACE study was designed to generate data that would help answer the question: "If risk factors for disease, disability, and early mortality are not randomly distributed, what influences precede the adoption or development of them?" This data would then provide previously unavailable scientific information that could be used to develop more effective prevention programs. By taking a whole life perspective, the ACE Study uncovered how childhood stressors are strongly related to the development and prevalence of risk factors for disease and social well being, throughout the human lifespan.[7]

These findings are important not only from a medical perspective. They also provide social and economic insights into how we become what we are as individuals and as a nation. As we struggle to understand mental and physical health crises that go beyond what even seems conceivable in a *developed* country, the ACE Study becomes a key piece of the puzzle. It helps to explain not only the prevalence of these conditions, but their almost eerie persistence in our culture (recall the statistics on anxiety cited at the beginning of Chapter 1) in spite of medical services that are considered by many to be the most advanced anywhere in the world. Indeed, the time factors in the study, among a large population of middle-aged, middle class Americans (the average age of participants was 57), make it clear that time did *not* heal many common adverse childhood experiences. So it turns out that unresolved emotional pain and trauma is not only the underlying cause of a broad range of psychological and physical health problems, but even worse, many people do not and cannot *just get over it* naturally, with the passing of time.

---

7 Adapted from Adverse Childhood Experiences Study,
   www.cdc.gov/nccdphp/ace/pyramid.htm.

> Emotional problems are often
> the sinister force behind not only
> psychological problems, but
> physiological ones as well.

Among the study's findings was the discovery that a huge number of adult conditions—including heart disease, diabetes, obesity, alcoholism, hepatitis, fractures, occupational health, and job performance—are all directly associated with childhood traumas. The study also found a strong correlation with mental and emotional problems such as anxiety and depression. And one rather shocking discovery was that the number of *distinct categories* of childhood traumas someone endured has a direct correlation with the rate of prescriptions for psychotropic drugs. In other words, the more varied, severe, and repeated the childhood traumas, the more likely that someone will suffer from conditions requiring these drugs, like anxiety and depression.[8]

Of course, the ACE Study merely confirms what many

---

8 The ACE Study developed a "score" by grouping adverse childhood experiences into eight general categories and then noting the number of distinct categories each participant had been exposed to. The categories were: (1) recurrent physical abuse; (2) recurrent emotional abuse; (3) sexual abuse; (4) living with an alcoholic person or a drug user; (5) family member in prison; (6) family member chronically depressed, mentally ill, or suicidal; (7) mother treated violently; (8) parents separated, divorced, or in some way absent during childhood. There was a direct, graded correlation between Ace Score and adult pharmacy costs, number of doctor office visits, emergency department use, hospitalization, and death.

of us who work in the healing arts have known intuitively for a long time: emotional problems are often the sinister force behind not only psychological problems, but physiological ones as well. The graded correlations (that is, more childhood trauma equals a higher incidence of adult physical and mental health problems) of the ACE Study, with its large population and high statistical significance, finally prove what we have suspected to be true all along. And while this may be depressing news to the medical industry with its reliance on the treatment of symptoms, it is in fact heartening to those of us working in the field of **Human Software Engineering**.

The reason is this: While the ACE Study demonstrates that adult health risks can be the direct result of childhood trauma and proves that the emotional fallout from these traumas is highly resistant to self-healing, it fails to address one extremely important point: Why? That is, *why* are these adverse experiences so resistant to self-healing? After all, if you cut your finger, the finger will heal in a week. If you break your leg, the pain may be intense, and the recovery time may be a month or more. But eventually, the pain subsides, the bone heals, and for all intents and purposes, you're "over it."

If the body is in many cases so good at healing itself, why is this not the case with the mental trauma of these adverse childhood experiences? The results of the ACE Study make it clear that new methods are needed for resolving the resistance to self-healing so that the long-term impact of these childhood traumas can be mitigated, but it does not answer what is, in effect, the million-dollar question. Why?

> If the body is in many cases so good at healing itself, why is this not the case with the mental/emotional trauma of adverse childhood experiences?

The solution to this riddle may be simpler than it first appears, and this is why we in field of **Human Software Engineering** can be heartened by the results of the ACE Study. If one considers that the *Core Dynamics* model of preverbal conditioning can explain how we unwittingly create the conditions that cause us to resist healing from emotionally traumatic events, it is certainly plausible that this preverbal conditioning can create a kind of preliminary layer in the ACE pyramid that comes before the traumas and actually causes the inability to self-heal. Without the layer of preverbal conditioning, the adverse childhood experiences would be much like breaking your leg—painful, even traumatic, but ultimately healed by good care and the passage of time.

I have added an additional layer at the base of the ACE Pyramid. My experience shows that preverbal conditioning, which we have identified as the key to many of our emotional difficulties in adult life, also preconditions us to resist healing from the kinds of adverse childhood experiences that are detailed in the ACE Study. It sets us up to try to escape from the pain created by the residual effects of unresolved traumas. The important layer of information added to my own work by the ACE Study is the possibility that this same preverbal conditioning might actually be putting our health at risk, and even cause early death. That is why I feel so heartened by the findings of the ACE Study. As the general public becomes aware that traumas resistant to self-healing can become the source of adult health risks, they will become more open to discovering ways to overcome that resistance, and truly heal their childhood traumas.

THE ACE PYRAMID, WITH THE ADDED LAYER

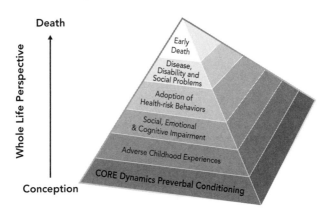

What I learned from the ACE Study confirmed my sense of urgency to get my message out into the world. If you are suffering from anxiety and you exhibit other destructive or escape-type behaviors, you have probably experienced more than one of the categories of adverse childhood experiences listed in the study. Using the techniques in Part II of this book to *Vaporize Your Anxiety* may therefore remove the need for the other behaviors and have a kind of very positive domino effect on your life.

After reading Dr. Felitti's article on the CDC website, I contacted him immediately. He agreed to meet with me so that we could discuss the possible relationship between the ACE Study and the work that I had been doing with **Human Software Engineering**. In a subsequent meeting, he allowed me to interview him about the ACE Study. The video of our interview is available in the Members Section of the *Vaporize Your Anxiety* website. You can watch it there, and check out all the other great resources at: www.vaporizeyouranxiety.com/resources.html

CHAPTER 4

The 12 Core Dynamics of Human Conditioning

> The Core Dynamics are the road map of the nature of preverbal human conditioning

Up to this point, we've focused on the concept of preverbal conditioning and feeling-level decisions without discussing the nature and specific effects of those decisions. There are twelve essential forms of preverbal conditioning that, when taken together, form what I call *The Core Dynamics of Human Conditioning.* The *Core Dynamics* are a set of penetrating insights into the nature of preverbal human conditioning. They were discovered after many years of inquiry and research while developing the field of **Human Software Engineering**. They are the basis for a new way of understanding the ways in which our past emotional conflicts, if left unresolved, continue to limit our present life.

There are many forms of preverbal conditioning. The main ones are summarized on a chart below. An expanded Venn diagram is used to show the interrelationships between each of these *Core Dynamics*.

THE 12 CORE DYNAMICS OF HUMAN CONDITIONING

Each Core Dynamic is the *expression* of one of those *feeling-level decisions* we made when we were very young. As we've discussed, these decisions were not made with words—they were preverbal and precognitive. When we grow up and acquire verbal and cognitive skills, we forget that we made these powerful feeling-level decisions, such as the decision to do our best to avoid being emotionally overwhelmed by shutting down our access to our own innate capacity to feel. So we are left with a series of limiting ideas and behaviors that are typically entrenched and unassailable through therapy. What the whole thing comes down to, however, is a conditioned response that keeps us in a perpetual state of underused potential.

In the case of anxiety, we have become especially good at avoiding fully feeling and thus resolving, the fear that is at its root. If you refer to the diagram above, you'll see that *Resisting Feeling Things Fully* is the central Core Dynamic, and I have found in my work that this is the primary core dynamic with which anxiety sufferers are dealing. The Core Dynamic of Resisting Feeling Things Fully tends to create people who become very *skilled* at this emotional-overwhelm-avoidance strategy. Unfortunately, this skill has also kept us in the perpetual low-grade experience that we call anxiety. And until we make some major breakthroughs around this fundamental way we have learned to function, we will typically stay stuck in it.

On the diagram, the three central *Core Dynamics* - Trying to Force an Outcome, Looking for Yourself Where You Are Not, and Resisting Feeling Things Fully - form the "operating system level" of our bugged inner human software. Each of these three central *Core Dynamics* has three primary expressions shown in the corresponding expanded oval. The corresponding nine *Core Dynamics* are considered our "office suite" of bugged application software.

The *Core Dynamics* model is a road map of the nature of our preverbal conditioning. But in order to understand how preverbal conditioning affects us, it will be useful to take a look at the basic structure of all human experiences.

THE THREE ASPECTS OF HUMAN EXPERIENCE

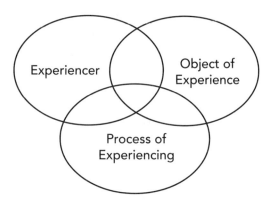

Every human experience has three fundamental components: The person having the experience, or the experiencer; the object of experience; and the process of experiencing. For example, if you listen to music, you are the experiencer; the music is the experience; and one or more of your senses (in this case hearing) is involved.

Together, these three aspects of experiencer, object of experience, and process of experiencing are essential to all of our experiences.

When we are very young, we have experiences that are too much for our delicate systems to process. Our mechanisms of experiencing are not yet developed enough to handle many of our experiences at this tender stage. As a result, we tend to become inappropriately identified with a mistaken interpretation of one or more of the three components of experience. And this is where problems begin.

If we identify too strongly with the object of our experience, we tend to develop the sense that some crucial part of ourselves is missing. For example, everyone has seen a baby crying and reaching out to its mother for comforting or to be held. Understandably, infants have a powerful feeling of total dependence on mom or others for their care. This naturally engenders a sense that I can't live without mom (or the mom function). This creates a visceral identification with mom. It feels like she is an essential part of who we are.

If we identify too strongly with our notions of who we think we are (the experiencer), we tend to develop the sense that we are our ego. This begins as we start to develop a sense of ourselves as a separate individual. We begin to want to have things our way. Think of the toddler who wants to keep playing instead of going to bed.

The battle of wills begins and may lead to a tantrum. We are already caught up in the illusion that we are the "doer," the "decider," the one who is going to will our life to be the way we want it to be!

If we identify too strongly with the process of experiencing, we will often end up being easily overwhelmed and afraid to feel things fully. When a small child riding in a shopping cart reaches for the candy bar on the grocery store checkout counter he or she will often get their hand swatted away or have "No!" barked at them by a tired mom. The ensuing emotional overwhelm produces a feeling level decision to just try to not feel so much. It's too painful. We can't handle it. It is in something this seemingly minor that the seeds of future anxiety are planted.

As the diagram that follows shows, identifying too strongly with any one of the three aspects keeps us from experiencing a sense of being whole and of feeling things fully. We will be cut off from the experience of *Pure Awareness*, our essential nature. And when we can't access the experience of who and what we really are, it is a natural set up for becoming anxious.

These three aspects of every experience are not independent. They all exist together. However, when the predominance of identification becomes emphasized between any two of them, we experience frustration, struggle and isolation. For example, if we tend to identify strongly both with a false sense of ourselves and with the object of our experience, we end up feeling frustration, because we are completely identified with our ego and at the same time feel strongly that some part of ourselves is missing. If we identify too strongly both with our false inner sense of self and the process of experiencing, we end up feeling like we're in constant struggle because the ego, which demands that its presence be recognized, is battling against the temptation to become absent in the face of strong emotions. If, on the other hand, we tend to over-identify with the object of our experience and the process of experiencing, we can feel terribly isolated, since we at once feel as though some part of ourselves is not there and we feel terrified of being overwhelmed.

THE ORIGIN OF PROBLEMS

You can probably relate to the feelings I just described in the last paragraph. And whether you have become identified with one, two or all three of these components of human experience, you'll tend to remain stuck, unable to become truly aware of the wholeness of your experiences. You'll tend to suffer under illusions, helpless to change things.

When we are very little, we make decisions about ourselves and about our experience of the world around us, even though we cannot yet express these decisions with language. These rudimentary decisions form the basis of our preverbal conditioning. Since language is not yet available to us—or is, at most, very under-developed, these decisions are made at the level of feeling. Language we may not have, but feelings we have in abundance. And it is these feeling-level decisions that become the basis of the 12 *Core Dynamics* of Human Conditioning.

> Understanding the nature of our preverbal conditioning by understanding the essence of the 12 Core Dynamics sheds light on exactly how our conditioning operates to keep us absorbed and lost inside the grip of our life experiences and our anxieties about them.

This understanding also helps us to begin to appreciate the invisible, unconscious quality of the conditioning. In addition, it helps us to understand when and why to use the eight *Pure Awareness* Techniques as the antidotes to being caught up in and lost to our illusions that the *Core Dynamics* create. The following is a description of the basic insights into the nature of the conditioning of each of the 12 *Core Dynamics* of Human Conditioning.

THE CORE DYNAMICS

To fully understand The *Core Dynamics*, you must first accept that we are each born perfect. We each have within us, at birth, *Pure Awareness*, and before the people with whom we are surrounded and the environment in which we live begin to impact us, we are replete with potential and possibility. As we come into contact with others, however, and as our environment begins to affect us, that potential becomes shrouded, our *Pure Awareness* is clouded by what we have come to call The *Core Dynamics*. And it is in understanding these Dynamics and then peeling them away that we can once again reach our *Pure Awareness*, the essence of who we are, and all our potential.

RESISTING FEELING THINGS FULLY

This Core Dynamic is based on the experience of being emotionally overwhelmed when we are very young and making a feeling-level decision to attempt to not feel intense emotional experiences fully. It was the best response that we could come up with at the time. The fear of emotional overwhelm seems to be universal. In other words, everyone seems to make this preverbal decision. It just seems to come with the territory of being human. *The consequences of making this feeling-level decision are that we begin to build our life around strategies of avoidance in order to minimize the awful experience of being emotionally overwhelmed.* This Core Dynamic is at the heart of why we don't know how to resolve the fears underlying our anxiety.

The three primary expressions of these strategies that are also feeling-level decisions in and of themselves are:

· Ignoring Your Intuition
· Being Judgmental
· Avoiding the Present

IGNORING YOUR INTUITION

Just about everyone has experienced having intuitive insights and then not consistently trusting and acting on them. It is only later, when you discover that your intuition was right, that you could just kick yourself for not acting on it. Why do we do that?

After the feeling-level decision to resist feeling things fully is already in place, we have all kinds of experiences of doing things to explore life, our bodies, and the world around us. Sometimes these explorations meet with resistance from our parents or others. As explained earlier, if we draw a picture all over our bedroom wall with a felt-tip marker, we may be excited to share our creative self-expression with our parents, but they may not share our enthusiasm for what we have done. If we get punished for it, we may experience an array of overwhelming emotions such as feeling betrayed, bewildered, hurt, scared, fearful, and angry that our source of love, support and nurturing has turned on us. What could be more terrifying? And we have yet another experience of being emotionally overwhelmed.

It doesn't take having many experiences like this before we start to have the fear of negative consequences that will lead to emotional overwhelm immediately following any intuitive or creative impulse that may come to us. This cultivates the habit of NOT trusting or acting on our intuition. It also cultivates the fear of confrontation, the fear of standing up for yourself, and the fear of being true to yourself, especially under any circumstances where there's the possibility of someone being upset with us for what we do.

BEING JUDGMENTAL

Most of us grow up in an environment in which people are judgmental of themselves and others. We learn this by observation of this behavior modeled by others. But there's more to it than that. The phenomenon of being judgmental is a way of resisting feeling things fully. Sometimes we have a feeling inside of ourselves that we don't want to feel, something that makes us uncomfortable. It can be triggered by observing someone who is displaying a behavior that is similar to a behavior of our own with which we are uncomfortable.

It is easier to see it in someone else. It is also easier to judge it as something bad or wrong in them than admit that this is also something inside of us. We don't want the feeling of our own discomfort with our own behavior, so we develop a tendency to express our distaste, our judgmental feelings, toward the other person or situation rather than recognizing that the feeling is really inside of ourselves. The charge that is the energy of being judgmental is inside of us, not over there in the other person. Whether we are judging someone else or judging a part of ourselves, the result is the same; we use it as a strategy so that we don't have to feel strong overwhelming feelings that are inside of us.

It is the entire phenomenon of avoidance of our own inner feelings of discomfort through being judgmental that is modeled for us and which we become conditioned to adopt. After all, it seems to us like being judgmental is just a part of how people are.

AVOIDING THE PRESENT

When we resist feeling things fully, we have a tendency to not complete intense emotional experiences. In our attempt to avoid emotional overwhelm, we archive the residue of these unresolved intense emotional experiences. This causes us to accumulate a database of patterns of unresolved, incomplete emotional energy in our bodies. It's called "emotional baggage" or the pain-body. Everyone has it in varying degrees. This is because the Core Dynamic of Resisting Feeling Things Fully is so universal.

The result of having a database of incomplete emotional energies held in our body is that when we allow ourselves to be fully present, the patterns of energy of the incomplete experiences begin to press into our awareness, demanding to be felt and completed. But we don't want to feel them. We're afraid of being overwhelmed by them so we adopt behaviors of avoiding the present so that we don't have to face this fear or experience the residual emotional pain from the past. This leads to the use of mood-altering substances and all kinds of addictive behaviors in order to self-medicate to avoid the pain. This is the real underlying basis of addictions. Some of these addictions can be as simple as absorbing ourselves in stories about the past or the future just to stay out of the present where the potential of having to face and feel the pain of the past seems like a dangerous thing to do.

LOOKING FOR YOURSELF WHERE YOU ARE NOT

This conditioning occurs within the first days and weeks after we are born. It is caused by the combination of our complete dependence on others for getting our needs met and being identified with our mother. Mom still feels like a part of us even after the umbilical cord is cut. This combination of dependence and identification makes us feel that when a need doesn't get met quickly enough, rather than saying, "Hey, where's mom? This is awful! She's not meeting my need. I don't know if I'll survive if my need doesn't get met," we make a feeling-level conclusion that it is a part of ourselves that is missing. Of course we don't have language yet, but we do interpret such experiences by making the feeling-level decision that "part of me is missing"—and it's the part of me that meets my needs.

This, again, seems to be quite universal. Having our needs not met in a timely way happens even in the best of households. It seems that everyone develops the tendency to feel like a part of himself or herself is missing to one degree or another. This leads to a pervasive feeling that if I could just get my needs met, then I'd finally feel whole and complete. So we chase after goals and desires with an undercurrent of hope that when the goal is reached or the desire is fulfilled, it will finally make us feel whole and complete.

But the problem is that no amount of love, attention,

money, time, possessions, experiences—no amount of anything - can possibly make us feel whole and complete. This is because we already are whole and complete, so there's nothing missing to begin with. But it doesn't FEEL like we're whole. It feels like we won't be whole and complete unless we get the right romantic partner, or the perfect job, or the sports car, or the house with an ocean view. When we reach these goals, expecting these accomplishments and acquisitions to bring us lasting fulfillment, how long does the sense of fulfillment actually last? Not very long because there isn't anything that can satisfy this longing for a sense of completion. But, we keep trying, thinking that the next thing will finally do it for us. What's really missing is the direct experience of what we really are, our essential nature—*Pure Awareness*. As you'll soon see, the experience of *Pure Awareness* provides the very experience of being whole and complete that we've been longing for all of our lives.

The Core Dynamic - Looking For Yourself Where You Are Not - gives rise to its three primary expressions:

· Mistaking Need For Love
· Resisting Change
· Limiting Self-Expression

MISTAKING NEED FOR LOVE

Due to the nature of the Core Dynamic of Looking For Yourself Where You Are Not, we are so intent on making sure that our needs get met that the meeting of needs becomes confused with the experience of love. In truth, however, getting a need met is simply getting a need met. It doesn't really have anything to do with love. We become conditioned to think that love means getting needs met. "If you loved me, you would ..." (meet my need). But feeling loved is just a variation on feeling whole and complete. Love is actually more of a state of being than it is something that you give or get from others.

When you experience *Pure Awareness*, you are experiencing a state of pure love. It is the only thing that truly is love; it is unconditional love. That means that love isn't dependent upon anything outside of you. You naturally love unconditionally by simply being in the state of pure love that is the same as *Pure Awareness*. The only *true* form of love is unconditional. Everything else is need.

We've all heard the old saying that you cannot love someone else until you love yourself. We also hear that you cannot look to someone else for happiness; that happiness has to come from within. In a simplistic way, this is what mistaking need for love is all about.

Saying that love and *Pure Awareness* are the same may seem a bit abstract, and it is, especially until you have had the direct experience of *Pure Awareness*. Because we can only relate to words in relation to the experiences that we have already associated with them, the comparison of unconditional love to *Pure Awareness* can't make real sense to you until you have had a taste of *Pure Awareness*. So after you go through the GAP Technique and have had a clear experience of *Pure Awareness*, I suggest that you read these few paragraphs about the distinction between love and need again. You will find that after experiencing *Pure Awareness* directly, the idea that it is also a state of pure unconditional self-love will begin to make sense to you.

RESISTING CHANGE

We all want to have a stable, secure and safe foundation for our lives. As such, we like to have things that we can depend upon, things that don't change. However, *there isn't anything in creation that isn't changing, even if the changes are sometimes imperceptible.* What we are really looking for, usually without knowing it, is the only real unchanging state of being that exists. That state of being—*Pure Awareness*—as you will see when using the GAP Technique is the unchanging nature of our own inner essence. There's nothing there *to* change. You need duality and diversity to have change. In *Pure Awareness*, there is only Awareness itself. *Pure Awareness is the only stable unchanging reference that it is possible to have.* And using the *Pure Awareness* Techniques, you can rapidly cultivate a state of being in which the awareness of *Pure*

Awareness is always present and never lost. This is the only real state of stability that is possible.

In the absence of the experience of *Pure Awareness*, what happens is that we do a special form of Looking For Yourself Where You Are Not. We become identified with things in our lives that SEEM like they are not changing. We become attached and identified with anything that has simply been around for a long time. Our old, unresolved emotional pain can have this quality of feeling. In fact, anything that seems like it has been around for a long time can become a source of identification: your job or career, if you had it for a long time; your name; your status or degree; your body; your reputation; your home, spouse or children; your habits and conditioning; your ideology or beliefs or religion. But none of these are things that are truly non-changing. These things are all subject to change and, to the degree that you are getting part of the sense of yourself from any of them; you will resist change in order to protect your sense of self.

LIMITING SELF-EXPRESSION

If part of the sense of who we are is coming from the feeling of being connected to our friends and family, and if most of these people are not powerfully self-expressed in the world (which is usually the case), then we may have a tendency to hold ourselves back from being fully self-expressed in the world ourselves. We will unknowingly participate in a game that we might call "Let's all stay mediocre together!" This Core Dynamic, Limiting Self-Expression, is an expression of Looking For Your Self Where You Are Not because it causes us to NOT start that new business or NOT write that book we've been meaning to write, etc. Limiting Self-Expression also tends to keep us from living from *Pure Awareness* all the time because we are identified with the false sense that our connection with others, having them like us, accept us, or approve of us, is something that we can't afford to be without.

Limiting Self-Expression also expresses itself as the fear that others, even people we don't know, will disapprove of us or our creative expression. We're afraid that people will take pot shots at us. "What if they don't like my book?" "What if someone criticizes my creative expression?" We end up operating from a place where "I'll just hold back and not put it out there and then I don't have to be at risk."

[
Strangely enough, the reason that people don't want us to be powerfully self-expressed or successful is that it puts it in their face that they are playing small.
]

Our powerful self-expression in the world is something they don't want to see because it reminds them that they are not living up to their own potential. They don't want to be reminded of that.

> Our fear is that it will be "lonely at the top" because others will pull away from us if we are truly successful.

The reality, however, is that it's not lonely at the top. When you are powerfully self-expressed, you just hang out with new friends who are also being powerfully self-expressed.

TRYING TO FORCE AN OUTCOME

This central Core Dynamic is the result of being conditioned to feel that we are our ego. It happens just by growing up in an environment where everyone feels that they are the collection of their life stories, accomplishments, disappointments, traumas, pleasures and all of their other experiences. This modeling seeps into us by osmosis. After all, if everyone is going around believing that they are the collection of their life experiences, there isn't really any other frame of reference available from which to learn.

The consequence of this conditioning is that we feel isolated. We feel separate from and at odds with the universe. This isolation causes us to feel that if something is going to happen, then I better make it happen. This is the illusion of being "the doer." It is the illusion of "authorship of action." For those who have the idea that, "I create my reality," the very mention of the idea of "the illusion of being the doer" sounds strange. "Of course I'm the doer. I can make my life happen the way that I want it to." This is the powerful voice of this conditioning.

Everyone has had the experience of having a desire, forgetting about it, and then having the desire fulfilled without seeming to have had to take any action at all. This is because in actuality the laws of nature are doing everything, even when it seems that our body, mind and personality are involved in the process. It is only our identification with our body, mind, personality, thoughts, actions, etc. that causes us to believe that we are "the doer," that we are an individual.

> But when you experience Pure Awareness, you find that what you are at your essence isn't your body, your mind, your thoughts, your experiences, your personality, your opinions, etc. You are limitless pure potential to be and experience anything.

Think for a moment about the experience referred to as being in the zone. This concept is frequently talked about in relationship to sports. When someone is playing in the zone, time slows down, everything is effortless, it seems almost like you are not doing it (and you're not, by the way). It's happening to you and through you, rather than you doing it. This is just what happened in those times when you had a desire, didn't do anything yourself to make it happen, and the result of your desire just showed up, without you doing anything. That's being in the zone. That's being in sync with the universe.

The universe operates on a law called The Law of Least Action, also sometimes called The Law of Least Effort. The planets travel around the sun in a path of least effort, an ellipse, not a square or rectangle. This law of least effort is what is operating as plants grow. It's the law that causes electrons to spin around the nucleus of an atom. It governs the rise and fall of the tides and every other natural process. Everything in nature happens with least effort and in perfect timing. This includes everything that happens to us as well. However, our conditioning of thinking and feeling that we are an isolated individual "doer" creating our reality causes us to force and struggle and suffer in trying to "make it happen" MY WAY and IN MY TIME!

Forcing things to happen your way or in your time may result in superficially seeming to get what it is that you think you want.

It is our identification with our ego that causes us to attempt to coerce life into showing up the way we want it to.

When we think and feel that we are separate from the rest of the universe, that we are isolated and alone, then we really can't help but try to make things happen the way that we think they should. However, our inability to sense the natural timing of things, our over-riding urge to try to control how things happen, causes us to attempt to force outcomes. What is needed is to learn to relax and allow life to show up in its own perfection and natural effortless timing. However, this is something that we are deeply conditioned not to do. Thus, we struggle and suffer needlessly because we are out of sync with the law of least effort.

There is an important distinction between doing things and forcing. For example, there is an important distinction between forcing and being persistent. Forcing involves attempting to coerce life into being some way that we think it *should* be. Persistence is simply sticking with something until it gets done because it needs sustained or repeated attention until completion. That's very different. It is not that we are not active. Think of it as being in "the zone." Like with sports, being in the zone doesn't mean to sit it out on the bench. You are in dynamic activity, but the inner experience of the activity is the antithesis of forcing. It is effortless, powerful, effective. This is what it means to be aligned with the law of least effort. It is powerful dynamic activity that has that effortless, in-the-zone quality to it. What a great way to live!

It also doesn't mean that we don't continue to learn, grow, improve our skills, our knowledge, etc. Whether you are studying in school or taking training at work or doing your own self-development by doing things like learning the techniques in this book, continuing to grow and evolve is also not forcing outcomes. And studying, learning and growing can all be done in that effortless zone-like way.

Trying To Force An Outcome expresses itself as:

· Excluding Other Perspectives
· Manufacturing Interpretations
· Over-reacting to Circumstances

EXCLUDING OTHER PERSPECTIVES

This expression of Trying To Force An Outcome occurs when we are identified with the way we see the world. This Core Dynamic is where bigotry and prejudice live. It is the source of most disagreement, fighting and wars in the world. It is expressed in all forms of fundamentalism. This is the real basis of religious wars, ethnic and racial discrimination, and much of the inability of people to get along with each other collectively, as well as in individual relationships.

When you become identified with your perspective, your particular beliefs become part of your self-definition. They really are not who you are, but they compellingly feel like they are a part of you. This makes you very vulnerable to having your sense of self feel threatened if you allow yourself to be open to seeing things in a new or different way. Your way becomes the only way, not only for you, but for everyone. "My way or the Highway!" You can't afford to be open to another way of seeing things, as it is too much of a threat to your very sense of your existence. So you stay closed-minded and isolated, feeling that you are right and wondering why all the other stupid people in the world don't see things like you do. They are heretics and unbelievers. I'm right and they are wrong. I need to be right in order to maintain the sense of my self.

MANUFACTURING INTERPRETATIONS

We all know people who have been adversely affected in the past and can't get over it. The event is long gone, but the stories about the event live on in the mind of the person, so much so that they are living inside of their story and cannot be fully present. They can also live in a story about how things will be in the future, either positive or negative. Whether the story is about the past or the future, it absorbs their attention and occupies their mind, and it seems like the story is a part of who they are.

> Attempting to make meaning of our experiences is a very human thing to do. But when we become identified with the stories that we make up about our experiences and live in these stories as if the events were still impinging upon our life, we are then no longer present to the reality of what is.

This is an obvious block to living in *Pure Awareness* all the time. Most people spend so much of their time trying to understand and make sense of their experiences that they rarely live in the present moment. This conditioning is identification with our thinking and intellect. It isn't possible to simply stop being absorbed in our stories just because we understand that we do this and decide not to. The conditioning will dominate your experience and you'll tend to be caught up in the stories until you learn how to experientially extract your awareness from being identified with the story. The *Pure Awareness* Techniques will teach you how to do this.

OVER-REACTING TO CIRCUMSTANCES

When we become overly identified with our stories, we start to expect life to show up the way that we think it should. Our expectations are created out of stories that we make up in our mind that are disconnected from reality. Whenever we are caught up in an expectation, we are living in the illusion that the universe will organize life the way that we want it to. When it doesn't, we tend to over-react with anger, disappointment, or a wide range of other possible emotions. This over-reaction keeps us absorbed inside of the energy of our emotional reaction. We stay identified with the expectation, the story out of which the expectation has been made, and to our "legitimate" emotional reaction. As you will see when you learn and experience the SEE *Pure Awareness* Technique, the expectation, story and emotional reaction are all illusions that we get lost to. You will experience how liberating it is to extract yourself from such identifications and experience yourself as your essential nature—*Pure Awareness*.

CHAPTER 5

Why the *Core Dynamics* Are Important

The *Core Dynamics* provide us with penetrating insights into why and how we get lost to the illusions created by our conditioning. You will see, as we progress through the book, why each *Pure Awareness* Technique is needed to guide you back from the particular kind of illusion you have become lost to, and precisely how to come out of the grip of the anxiety that this produces. You are about to embark on a great journey, perhaps one of the most important ones of your life. You are about to learn and experience not only who and what you really are, but also how you can live in an awakened state every moment for the rest of your life in which the possibility of anxiety simply doesn't exist.

Every experience we have in our life has both the circumstances that we find ourselves in and our reaction to those circumstances. Many times we can't do much, if anything, about the circumstances. But we can learn how to do something about our reactions to those circumstances.

Each Core Dynamic is a description of a particular way in which you have become lost to an illusion that you are separate from life itself, that you are an isolated individual. By understanding the essence of each of the *Core Dynamics*, you can then see what is needed in order to extract yourself from your conditioning and re-establish the direct experience of wholeness. And we have methods for doing this.

For example, the Core Dynamic of Resisting Feeling Things Fully needs a method of being able to do the opposite of this deep-seated conditioning, a method that will enable you to deflate your resistance and embrace feeling. Instead of staying stuck in the energy of unresolved feelings or emotional reactions caused by unmet expectations, you can use the CORE and SEE Techniques to accomplish this.

When you are absorbed in the kind of conditioning that causes you to look outside of yourself for validation, respect, love, attention, etc., in other words when you are caught in the Core Dynamic of Looking for Yourself Where You Are Not, the real need is to look for yourself where you are! You can experience this by using the GAP and AGAPE Techniques to experience that who and what you are is already whole and complete and that you don't need anything from outside of yourself to validate your wholeness.

What is most important is to understand that every type of conditioning is a problem at an experiential level. These are not intellectual problems. They are problems with the way in which you experience life. This is why the *Pure Awareness* Techniques are all experiential, not intellectual.

With the insights of the Core Dynamics and the liberating effects of the Pure Awareness Techniques, you can readily resolve your conditioned reactions and come back to a place of clarity and calm so that you can then make decisions about your life that are really aligned with what is best for you.

Every experience we have in our life has both the circumstances and our reaction to those circumstances.

Many times we can't do much, if anything, about the circumstances. But we can learn how to do something about our reactions to those circumstances. When you are caught up in the emotion of your reaction, it's very difficult to even see the circumstances clearly, not to mention being able to respond to them in a way that is beneficial to you. With the insights of the *Core Dynamics* and the liberating effects of the *Pure Awareness* Techniques, you can readily resolve your conditioned reactions and come back to a place of clarity and calm so that you can then make decisions about your life that are really aligned with what is best for you.

There is a synergy between the *Core Dynamics* and the *Pure Awareness* Techniques. As the *Core Dynamics* provide *insights* into the details of how you become identified with everything that you are not, the *Pure Awareness* Techniques provide the *experiential pathways* back to the direct experience of what you truly are. Whether it is simply experiencing your essential nature via the GAP Technique or coming out of the grip of an emotional reaction with the SEE Technique or the Core Technique, all of the *Pure Awareness* Techniques bring you out of your illusions of separateness and back to the direct experience of your essential nature.

When you find that you are unhappy with your life or that you are caught up in problems or reactions or anxiety, understanding of the *Core Dynamics* can always provide a distinction between what is happening and your reactions to what is happening. Whenever you are stuck in life, take a look at the *Core Dynamics* Model and see which of the 12 *Core Dynamics* is being expressed. It can be just one of the dynamics or several of the dynamics at play. Then use the appropriate *Pure Awareness* Technique to bring yourself back to the experience of your essential nature. This is how to ***Vaporize Your Anxiety*** and create a way of being in which you never have to suffer from anxiety again.

CHAPTER 6

Debugging the *Core Dynamics* of Human Conditioning

> The fundamental breakthrough we need to make, then, is to let go of our conditioned avoidance response, and truly make the decision to feel things fully

In order to truly vaporize anxiety, the fundamental breakthrough we need to make is to let go of our conditioned avoidance response and truly make the decision to feel things fully. In fact, in part two of this book, you'll learn two simple, experiential techniques that allow you to finally learn to use more of your full capacity to feel. The SEE Technique and the CORE Technique are powerful ways to resolve the underlying fears at the basis of your anxiety. They both teach you new ways of utilizing your innate capacity to feel so that you can effectively resolve these fears rather than just avoid them, mask them, stuff them, or numb them with medications or drugs.

As you'll see when you begin using these techniques, they are elegant, simple, and powerful ways to liberate yourself from the grip of your anxiety and other negative emotions as well.

As I described in Chapter 2, when we're cut off from our innate capacity to feel things fully, we tend to leave the experience of intense feelings incomplete. Carrying around these accumulated incomplete emotional experiences creates *emotional baggage*—the old, unresolved, painfully intense feelings that we travel with every day, often without even knowing it. Most of us have *suitcases* full of emotional pain we carry around with us, unaware that we could just… toss it out. We may be able to successfully distract ourselves from these feelings for a while—even, as I've suggested, by getting really good at being anxious! But whenever life settles down for a few moments, there they are, pressing up to the surface, wanting to be felt and healed.

People become resigned to this state, and assume that this must just be *how life is*. After all, we have no other frame of reference. We can only know that which we have experienced. Think about it: so many of us live with anxiety, nervousness, and depression on a *daily basis*. And we think it's normal. Or if we don't, we assume there's no alternative that doesn't involve medication. Of course, this is a logical assumption, given the nearly universal beliefs that we can't handle *too much emotion*. (That's okay—we can just take a pill!) This belief really *feels as if it's true*, because we've spent our whole lives conditioned to resist feeling things fully. So it's hard to believe it could be otherwise. But the truth is, *it's not the truth!*

[
The good news is that you can handle all the emotions you will ever encounter, in their complete and unadulterated intensity.
]

As we discussed earlier, neuro-scientific research has proven that as adults we have acquired all the spindle cells necessary to process our emotions, even the painful and terrifying ones. The problem is, we're still operating based on a three year-old's unwitting decision to avoid feeling things fully.

In other words, we have the right *hardware*, but our *software* or *operating system* is so full of bugs that we can't handle robust emotional experiences. It's kind of like having a modern computer with tons of memory and a powerful processor, but running on an operating system from 1985. You can keep expanding the memory and buying faster processors, but until you update the operating system, you'll never be able to realize the computer's true potential. When you finally *do* update the operating system and get rid of those bugs, all of a sudden, your computer runs like a dream.

> Our inner human software operating system needs to be upgraded, from a state in which we are operating on the fear of being overwhelmed to a state of being in which we can access and fully utilize our innate capacity to feel.

Likewise, when our lives are being run by the *Core Dynamics*, no amount of intellectually advanced, streamlined thinking can get us out from under their spell. Instead, our inner human software operating system needs to be upgraded. We need to upgrade from a state in which we are operating on the fear of being overwhelmed to a state of being in which we can access our innate, if unused, capacity to feel. This will allow us to learn how to experience the energy of emotions in our body to completion, without the fear of being overwhelmed by them.

NO MORE FREEZES!

Have you ever noticed that anxiety has the effect of making you feel like you can't take action—even if you know exactly what action you should take? When anxiety is intense, it's almost like you freeze. We all know what it's like when our computer freezes, right? Well, it's very much the same with anxiety. When you're plagued by the bugs in your inner human software that create anxiety you simply get stuck, and often the only way to get past it is to *shut down* and *reboot*. The conundrum with that strategy is that when you restart, the problem is still there, waiting to show up (in the form of anxiety) when confronted with a triggering experience.

What you will experience in the second half of this book is a way to debug your inner software so that you *won't* freeze when you encounter anxiety-triggering situations. You will literally upgrade your inner human software by learning to feel things completely. You will learn how to join the three components of every human experience—the experiencer, the object of experience, and the process of experiencing—so that you can operate from a state of integration and wholeness. As you will see, it is not only possible to be completely free from anxiety; it's much easier than you think. I invite you, then, to come along as we dive into the practical application of the anxiety vaporizing techniques that I've developed. You're closer than you think to freedom from anxiety!

As you practice the *Pure Awareness* Techniques that you learn from this book, you will be dismantling the limitations of your preverbal childhood conditioning in ways that are incredibly effective. You will begin to come out of the grip of your conditioning. You will begin to live a whole new kind of life, a life that is free of the invisible binding influences of the *Core Dynamics*. When the *Core Dynamics* are thoroughly absent, you live with the lively presence of *Pure Awareness* all the time. Here's what life is like when the *Core Dynamics* are gone.

THE ABSENCE OF THE CORE DYNAMICS OF HUMAN CONDITIONING

CHAPTER 7

What is *Pure Awareness*?

> Pure Awareness is the experience
> of awareness itself.

Pure Awareness is the experience of awareness itself. It is the experience of awareness without the experience of being aware of an object of experience. This is a unique experience as we are usually aware of objects of perception. It is important to be able to access and directly experience *Pure Awareness* because this is the experience of pure presence. It is the experience of living fully in this moment, in the *now*.

Anxiety occurs when we find ourselves living in experiences or stories about the past or future. *Pure Awareness* is of our essential nature. That means that it is the part of us with which we experience everything else.

By using the *Pure Awareness* Techniques you can gradually cultivate a state of being in which *Pure Awareness* is present all the time. In this state of being, anxiety simply doesn't exist.

Pure Awareness is the life force at the center of my work in the field of **Human Software Engineering**. When you use the CORE Technique to feel down into the energy of a feeling, all the way to completion, you may have a sense of the energy dissipating or dissolving, almost like the fog burning off in the morning sun. As that fog lifts off what's left is... nothing. Even though there is nothing of the energy of the emotion left to experience, this nothingness has some special characteristics. If you have already experienced this you know that the nothingness feels expansive, peaceful, calm, awake, lively and soothing.

This is the direct experience of your own awareness. I sometimes call this *the awareness of awareness,* because there is nothing that you are being aware *of* at that moment. Most of the time we are not aware of awareness because our awareness is busy *being aware* of some object of our experience. We are used to experiencing *things* with our awareness, not *nothingness*. But with these techniques, when you are in the state of *Pure Awareness* there *is* no object of experience. There is only awareness itself. This wonderful experience is called *Pure Awareness*. When you do the GAP Technique later in the book, you'll see that you arrive in the same place of expansion, peace and calm in a very simple, quick way.

All the techniques in this book are *Pure Awareness Techniques.* They provide you with different ways to reconnect with your own awareness, under different circumstances. They bring you back to a state of being whole and complete. They bring you back to the experience of the essential nature of what you really are. They are some of the simplest and most practical, yet most profoundly useful techniques you may ever learn in your lifetime. Admittedly, becoming aware of awareness itself can seem a bit strange at first. But you will find that this experience of *Pure Awareness* is quite wonderful. In *Pure Awareness*, there is no anxiety, no distress, only peace of mind and a deep sense that everything is just fine.

> We are used to experiencing things with our awareness, not nothingness.

When you begin to experience *Pure Awareness*, if there are things that have been troubling you, you will notice that although there may still be situations requiring your attention, there is a much clearer distinction between the situation itself and your old emotional reaction to it. *Pure Awareness* makes you better at dealing with life's challenges. It's tough to make decisions and take action when we are all wrapped up in our emotional reactions. But when you use the *Pure Awareness* Techniques to bring yourself back to the experience of awareness itself, you will stop being the victim of your emotions and begin to live more and more from a place of calm and clarity. You'll start to know what to do or even if anything needs to be done at all. You will start to live from the fullness of who and what you really are.

The real solution to anxiety is to transcend it—to extract yourself from the grip of emotion, and regain a state of inner peace and happiness. In other words, to cultivate a state in which anxiety simply does not and cannot exist. The key thing to remember is that your emotions are not *who you are*. *Pure Awareness* is who and what all of us *really* are.

> The real solution to anxiety is to transcend it—to extract yourself from the grip of emotion and regain a state of inner peace and happiness, to cultivate a state in which anxiety simply does not and cannot exist.

The truth is, these are not *difficult* techniques. It's only a matter of learning them and applying them when you need to. What is challenging is this: you have to *do* it. As we all know, *just doing it* is usually the hardest part. But if you simply allow yourself the time to practice the *Pure Awareness Techniques*, you'll quickly find yourself living from this exquisite state of being.

Pure Awareness is very simple. It is that attribute of you that is your awakeness, your aliveness. It is the screen of your mind upon which fall all of your thoughts and perceptions. It is your consciousness. It is that with which you experience everything.

Pure Awareness is so simple that we don't notice that it is there. Because *Pure Awareness* is not an object of experience itself, and is only in the background for our experiences, we don't normally notice that it is there. It's too simple, too silent, too... uninteresting!

Although most people are completely unaware that they have something called *Pure Awareness* within them, it is absolutely the most important part of us. It is our essential nature. It is our very aliveness. It is what gives us the ability to perceive and think and experience life.

Throughout recorded history, the experience of *Pure Awareness* has been a spiritual quest for untold thousands of seekers of truth. Meditation and other spiritual practices aspire to attain the direct experience of *Pure Awareness*. *Pure Awareness* goes by many names: Samadhi, Satori, Transcendental Consciousness, the Source, the Now, the Presence, the Absolute, Universality, Wholeness, and Enlightenment! The transcendentalist Ralph Waldo Emerson, Henry David Thoreau, Margaret Fuller, and others, attempted to describe it in their writings. Some authors on the subject describe having an experience of

Pure Awareness only to lose it and then struggle for years trying to recapture the experience again.

In the spiritual traditions of the world, people dedicate countless hours, days, years, and even lifetimes, to the pursuit of the experience of *Pure Awareness*. There are many disparate notions and a myriad of diverse practices, some of which are quite austere, that people have pursued for many years in the faint hope of catching a glimpse of *Pure Awareness*. And yet, as you will soon see, all that is needed is to look in the right place and you can experience it. It is so incredibly simple! Anyone can do this and have the experience of *Pure Awareness* in a moment. It's really that easy.

Vaporize your
ANXIETY

PART II
The Solution

CHAPTER 8

Is This a Form
of Therapy?

> The Vaporize Your Anxiety Program is a
> form of training—training in how to use
> your previously under-utilized ability to feel
> and resolve emotional pain and trauma

As we move into the second half of the book, I outline the practical application of the techniques we've been discussing and give you a roadmap for vaporizing your anxiety. But before we get there, I feel I should address one question I get a lot: Are the techniques described in this book a form of therapy? My response is that although it may have a wonderfully therapeutic effect—after all, it can vaporize anxiety and relieve deep-seated traumas and emotional pain—it is actually a form of *training*. Training, that is, in how to access and effectively utilize our previously underutilized capacity to feel. Everyone has this innate capability; we just haven't learned to use it.

This is similar to the development of the ability to read words silently and understand their meaning. Language formed from combinations of individual letters that each represent specific sounds developed about 2,500 years ago and is commonly attributed to the ancient Greeks. This was a major advance and simplification of the former Egyptian method of using hieroglyphics or pictures to represent spoken words. It made it much easier for people to learn how to read. However, initially all reading was done orally—by speaking the sounds of the letters and words out loud. For centuries most people had to read out loud in order to understand the meaning of words and sentences. The ability to read silently was unusual for most people and only became widely taught and practiced in the 20th century.

Imagine the amazement of the people who could only read out loud when they first encountered someone who was able to read words only inside their heads, and know their meaning. It must have seemed like a miracle! And yet now we take silent reading for granted. In fact, it's far more common than reading out loud. The truth is, human beings had the ability to read silently all along. They just didn't know they had it.

Likewise, we all have the innate ability to feel things fully. But just like the period before reading silently became the norm, we're now living in an era of human development in which our ability to access and use our innate ability to feel has been limited by our conditioning.

I would suggest that many of the problems people have are really caused by this inability to process their emotions. Perhaps once we become competent at doing this it will render the notion that we need therapy to resolve our problems obsolete. That's not to say that it won't take well-trained guides to help those who have severe issues that go beyond what you can learn from a book. And indeed, for people with severe psychological conditions, therapy may be necessary. But so called "normal" people—in other words, most of us—may only need to learn how to access and use our natural capabilities that have just lain dormant up until now.

So, again: Is this a form of therapy? I think not. Rather, it is a form of training; a form of education about how to use formerly underutilized parts of our natural abilities. If you are capable of feeling, you can learn to overcome the conditioning that makes you resistant to feeling, and you can learn to use these techniques to clean up your inner emotional and energetic landscape and *Vaporize Your Anxiety* as a natural consequence.

CHAPTER 9

The Practical Steps for Vaporizing Your Anxiety

Everyone who has anxiety would like to be free of it. You need a realistic strategy for dealing with anxiety-causing situations so that you can avoid slipping back into a pattern that makes you a victim of your emotional reactions. One strategy immediately available to you is to begin practicing the SEE and CORE Techniques, so that you'll quickly become good at them. By doing this, you'll gain the confidence that comes with knowing that *you can really feel any emotion fully* without become victimized by it. You'll get so used to using these techniques that as soon as you feel yourself slipping into an anxious state, your reflex will be to do the technique rather than to go into a full-blown state of anxiety.

If you've been suffering from Anxiety for some time, you have undoubtedly gotten pretty good at dancing around the edges of the energy of unresolved fears. Once you begin using the SEE and CORE Techniques, you may find a suitcase or more filled with them. You may need to do the techniques many times, because there are likely to be many patterns of energy of fears that haven't been completed. Then again, maybe you just have one big fear that you need to resolve. In either case, using the SEE and CORE techniques will allow you to vaporize the energy of the fear. Each time you complete an incomplete experience of one of the fears at the root of your anxiety or extract yourself from the grip of the fear coming from projecting a possible negative outcome onto the future, you'll notice that that situation doesn't trigger anxious feelings any more.

It is important to point out that the need to do the techniques many times is not because they don't work well. On the contrary, they work exceedingly well. And each time you use one, if you use it to the point where the energy of the fear is complete or has faded away completely, you won't have to deal with that one again. So the need for repeated use of the techniques is for resolving multiple fears that may be there at the basis of your anxiety, not because you have to keep using it on the same anxiety issue over and over again.

So let's begin. Here are the practical steps to get started
Vaporizing Your Anxiety:

1. Make a list of everything that causes you to feel
   anxious.

2. Learn the SEE Technique.

3. Learn the CORE Technique.

4. Use your list of anxiety-producing circumstances
   to give yourself access to the emotional energy
   of the fear that each issue produces. Simply by
   thinking about an item on the list you will usually be able to feel the anxious feeling.

5. Then immediately use the SEE and/or the CORE
   Technique to resolve the underlying energy of
   the fear in and/or around your body.

6. Learn the GPS Technique.

7. Use the GPS Technique to make sure that you
   have cleared out every possible energy of fear that
   produces anxiety for you associated with every
   item on your list.

8. Enjoy an anxiety-free life.

9. If any anxiety ever comes up for you again,
   simply use the SEE and CORE Techniques and
   vaporize it.

Although reading about and understanding these concepts are important preliminary steps, the SEE and CORE Techniques are really about *experiencing* them. These are very special, very particular kinds of experiences. To *get it* you need to *do it*. So I'd like to invite you to listen to some examples of people being guided through the SEE and CORE Techniques which I have recorded specially for readers of this book. After listening to these recordings, I'll give you a step-by-step description of how to do it. Just visit http://vaporizeyouranxiety.com/resources.html and you'll be able to listen to the recordings right on the website, or download them for playing on your computer or mp3 player.

CHAPTER 10

Making Your List

> Your list of things that make you anxious
> will help make sure that you resolve
> every trigger for your anxiety.

If you have listened to some examples of people being guided through the SEE and CORE Techniques, welcome back! If you did not have access to the examples, we will make the guidelines for how to do these techniques very clear in the book.

Now it is time to learn how to do it yourself.

The best way to start this process is by making a list of the things that make you anxious. If you are at all like me, when you read a book and the author gives you some exercise to do you may not feel like doing it and may even avoid doing it. But please don't skip this step! It's so important because in order to learn the CORE

Technique you're going to have to get in touch with the feelings that are the real core of your anxiety. This is an essential part of being able to learn and do the CORE Technique effectively.

So go ahead and get a piece of paper and write down at least of few of the things that you are anxious about. There may be one thing or just a few big things that are driving your anxiety. Or it may be that there are a whole bunch of them. Either way, making the list is going to be useful. So please do that now. If you'd like, go to www.vaporizeyouranxiety.com/resources.html and download a worksheet that will help you with this exercise. But if you're not at your computer, don't let that hold you back—a regular piece of paper and pen will do just fine!

If you're having trouble getting started, here are some things that others have said make them anxious. See if you can relate to any of these:

Job Security: My employer has been laying off workers and even though my job hasn't been affected yet the rumor going around the office is that there will be more layoffs. I really worry that I'll be one of the next ones to get that pink slip.

Public Speaking: I have to give a presentation to a group of people I've never met. I know my topic, but I have bad stage fright, and it's always worse when I don't know anyone in the audience. I'm concerned about how they are going to respond to me, and I'm worried I'll look ridiculous.

Parenting Issues: My teenage daughter has been out all night, and she didn't tell me that this was going to happen. It's 3:00 AM and she didn't take her cell phone with her.

Traumatic Event: Two months ago I had a car accident, and I can't seem to shake it. I'm recovered physically, but I'm terrified to drive.

Victimization: I was mugged last month, and it really scared me. I wasn't hurt or anything, but even though I know it's not rational, I just don't feel safe walking around by myself.

Personal Assault: I was raped several years ago. I have had great counseling, and the person who did it is in jail, but I can't get over it. I'm afraid it will happen again.

Relationship Issues: I was in an emotionally abusive relationship for two years. It's over now, but every time I meet someone new, I get so scared that it will happen again. I really want to start a new relationship, but I feel frozen.

Guilt by Association: One of my close coworkers was caught embezzling from our company. I had nothing to do with it, but I'm afraid I'll be guilty by association.

Natural Disaster: I was living in San Francisco when the earthquake hit in 1989. I don't live anywhere near a fault line now, but I'm still scared. I hold my breath every time I drive over a bridge.

Night Terrors: I have a lot of nightmares and scary thoughts. Sometimes I'm scared to go to sleep at night.

Negative Anniversaries: Every year, on the anniversary of the day I was attacked, I get so anxious I can hardly move.

Fear of Dying: Last year, out of the blue, my best man died suddenly—only three years after my wedding. He was in great health. I'm afraid something like that will happen to me.

Stagnation: I'm in a very dysfunctional, co-dependent relationship. I know what's wrong with it, but I'm afraid I don't have the willpower to end it. So I walk around anxious all the time.

Financial Issues: I'm in serious debt. I've tried so many things, and nothing helps. I think bankruptcy may be the only way out, but I'm scared that if I declare bankruptcy I'll be ostracized by everyone I know. I just feel frozen—I have no idea what to do.

Terrorist Attacks: I just heard the report on CNN about that terrorist attack, and I'm afraid we're next.

You may have your own variations of these items, or have completely different triggering situations in your life. Either way, take just 5 or 10 minutes to make your list (you can feel free to add to it at any time, of course). Try to be as specific as possible. For example, don't write, "Meeting new people makes me anxious." Instead, say something like, "When I met that nice single guy my friends invited to dinner, I got so anxious. It was like I couldn't even speak. It's weird, because I am smart and funny, and he obviously thought I was attractive. I don't know, I just froze." It's important to include as much detail as possible about these triggering situations, because that way, you'll really be able to hone in on the *precise* energy of the feeling in your body that is associated with the event. That is the key to success with the CORE Technique.

CHAPTER 11

Two Kinds of Fear at the Basis of Anxiety

> There are two kinds of fear. Projections of possible negative outcomes onto the future. Incomplete traumatically fearful experience from the past.

You are going to be learning how to do the SEE Technique and the CORE Technique to *Vaporize Your Anxiety*. They are each used on different kinds of fears. They can be also used for vaporizing other emotions as well.

There are two different categories of fears that underlie our anxiety. The primary kind is the fear that something will happen in the future that we can't handle or that will be very painful. The second kind of fear emanates from unresolved traumatic fearful experiences from the past. There is a third kind of fear but it's not at the basis of anxiety. That's appropriate fear that shows up in the present moment because there is something actually to be feared. For example, if you are standing on the railroad tracks and a train is coming at you, the body will start to generate the energy of fear to motivate you to get off of the tracks. This is entirely normal. This is appropriate fear. We don't want to get rid of this kind of fear as it is a powerful motivator to protect us from harm.

Notice that the fears at the basis of anxiety don't have anything to do with what is actually happening in the present moment. They are either projections of some kind of negative outcome onto the future, or they are unresolved emotional baggage from fearful experiences from the past. Either way, these fears are inappropriate. They cause us anxiety, and we tend to get stuck in them without the knowledge or resources to come out of their grip.

Now, however, we have discovered new experiential techniques that rapidly resolve both kinds of fear and the anxiety that they produce.

> For the kind of fear that is the projection of possible negative outcomes onto the future, we use the SEE Technique. For the incomplete traumatic fears from the past, we use the CORE Technique.

By far the most common form of fear that produces anxiety is the projection of possible negative outcomes onto the future. However, for forms of anxiety like Post Traumatic Stress Disorder (PTSD), the CORE Technique may be more commonly used as the source of the problems is mainly incomplete traumatic experiences from the past.

Sometimes the negative outcome is something specific like the fear of failing a test, or the fear that you'll get laid off in a downsizing, or the fear that you'll never meet the man or woman of your dreams. In all cases these are fears about something that has not yet happened.

Other times, projections of negative outcomes onto the future are more vague, such as the fear of uncertainty, or the fear of the unknown. In these cases the basic fear is that something might happen that you won't be able to handle.

Because the most common kind of fear that produces anxiety is from projecting negative outcomes onto the future, the SEE Technique will be the first technique to learn to *Vaporize Your Anxiety*.

CHAPTER 12

The SEE Technique: The Main Key to Freedom From Anxiety

> We become identified with our stories about the past and future. There is a field of emotional energy generated out of each of these stories. We live inside of the illusions produced by these energy fields that seem so compellingly real.

THE ENERGY FIELDS OF IDENTIFICATIONS, PROJECTIONS AND EXPECTATIONS

"Don't borrow trouble" is an expression you may have heard many times in your youth. Parents and grandparents tell it to children worried about school; adults tell it to other adults concerned about adult issues. But while we all espouse it, most of us don't live it. We worry, we fret, and we grow anxious about things that have not yet happened, that may never happen. And it is in this worry that we build our anxiety.

To deal with anxiety, the SEE Technique is particularly effective. To get you started, I'll first give you an explanation of the SEE Technique and how to do it. I will then give you a link to access audio examples on the Internet. In addition, I'll give you a script that you can use to practice the SEE Technique by having someone simply read the instructions to you while you sit comfortably with your eyes closed.

With each technique you will learn, it is important to open your mind to its possibilities and to take each step seriously. The techniques are extremely effective, but their effectiveness is dependent upon your ability and desire to see them through. The simplest way to begin the SEE Technique is to think of something that you are concerned about that might happen in the future. Even though this thing that you fear might happen at some point in the future hasn't happened yet, you are still feeling anxious about it.

Why would I go there on purpose, you may be asking yourself. Why would I borrow trouble? But it is important to immerse yourself in this fear so that you can learn to deal with it.

It is important here to notice that the emotion you are feeling can be experienced as a sensation of energy in and around your body. The sensation is simple to identify because if there were not any energy to the emotion, you would not be feeling it. Think of how sometimes tension and anxiety make us feel as though we are almost vibrating. It is that energy, at whatever level you are feeling it, that you need to address.

Once you recognize the energy of the feeling produced by the projection of the possible negative outcome onto the future—the thing about which you are anxious—you should be able let yourself notice where the energy of the emotion is coming from in your body. You may find it in your chest, belly or throat, but it could be anywhere. If it doesn't seem to be associated with a specific location, and you are not able to identify where it is coming from, that's OK too.

What *is* important is that you notice that the emotion is a field of energy. As you allow yourself to notice the entire field of the energy of this fear, you will find that it is not only located in your body but it also radiates outward into the environment surrounding you. It probably feels like it is surrounding you, engulfing you like an aura or cloud.

Typically, we don't allow ourselves to feel the whole energy field of our emotions. This is due to the conditioning that I described earlier as the Core Dynamic of Resisting Feeling Things Fully. In fact, some people learn to become disassociated from emotional energy. You may have developed a habit of going into your mind to try to figure something out, like why you feel this way or how could something like this happen. However, in the process that you are learning here, you are learning to shift your attention from the mind to the body, from thoughts about the sensation to experiencing the energy pattern of sensation itself.

> We want to distinguish our thoughts about the emotion from the sensation of the emotion in and around the body. For now, our interest is in the sensation of the emotion that is the experience of its energy field.

If you allow yourself to feel the entire field of the energy that your body is creating in its reaction to the projection of the negative outcome onto the future—the thing about which you are concerned—you may find that sometimes the energy field is quite large. It may extend outward from your body quite far. It may even be bigger than the room you are in; sometimes it is bigger than the entire world. When the fear of the possible negative outcome has been with you for a very long time, the energy field can sometimes seem like it is filling up your entire apparent universe. It may extend out beyond the solar system, the galaxy, all the out to the edge of the universe. Amazingly, it is possible to simply notice or sense how big it is, even when it is that big. But it is most likely that you haven't had anyone show you how to do that before.

The energy field of the emotion is occurring inside of your awareness. No matter how big the field of the energy is, it is always contained within your awareness. If the energy field really overwhelmed your entire field of consciousness, you would be unconscious. But you are conscious. You are reading this book and you are aware. Even when you are experiencing the field of energy of your projection or the possible negative outcome onto the future, you are aware. And it is your awareness that is making it possible to have that experience.

When you do the SEE Technique, you allow your awareness to expand.

You are starting from being inside of an energy field that is emanating from your body. In the SEE Technique, you are simply noticing how large the energy field is by allowing your awareness to expand outward from your body, just noticing if the energy of the emotional reaction is still there or not.

As you allow your awareness of the energy field to continue to expand, what you are looking for is the outer edge of the field of energy. Sometimes it will be clearly defined. Other times it will be vague or diffused like the evaporating edge of a cloud of mist. But whether it is clear or vague, when you come to the outer edge of the energy field you will be able to sense quietness just beyond the edge. The quietness will be clearly distinct from the energy of the fear. This quietness is your own awareness. It is that essential part of you that is allowing you to have this experience. It is the silent background in which the energy field is occurring. It is the same silent background of *Pure Awareness* that you will experience during the GAP Technique.

As you allow your awareness to notice the quietness out beyond the outer edge, you will begin to get a clear distinction between the energy field of the emotion and the silent background that contains it. In the moment that this distinction becomes clear, you have extracted your awareness from being collapsed inside of the energy field.

If you allow yourself to go more deeply into the quietness, further from the outer edge of the energy field, you begin to notice an increasingly clear distinction between the energy of the emotion and the background of silence in which the energy of the emotion is occurring. As you allow yourself to go even more deeply into the experience of the surrounding quietness, notice that there are no boundaries to it. It is vast and unlimited. It is also peaceful and calm. There is no fear, no anxiety here.

The SEE Technique takes us off to the side of the energy field to sense the silence in which it is occurring. This is just like noticing the silent background in which thoughts occur. But when you are caught up in an emotional reaction to the possibility of having to face some future negative experience, it is not so easy initially to find the background of silence. We typically get so absorbed in the experience of the fear, that to find the background of silence you have to take your awareness all the way out to the outer edge of the energy field of the fear. Then you can access the background of silence that is the quietness that surrounds it.

We are not used to doing this. It is the opposite of what we are conditioned to do. Instead, we are deeply conditioned to stay inside the energy field of our emotions. In my experience using this technique with thousands of people, I've observed that no one has ever had this experience before they learned the SEE Technique.

It is important to make clear that you can't get to the experience of that silent background of your own awareness with your intellect. You can't get there by thinking about it. It is an experience, not a thought. This is experiential, not intellectual. When you are experientially collapsed inside the energy field of your fear, you can't get out with your intellect. As long as you are in your mind thinking about it you will be stuck there inside of the energy field that is generated by those thoughts. The energy isn't intellectual, and just understanding that you are creating the energy in response to your projection of a possible negative outcome onto the future isn't going to liberate you from the energy field.

It may be of value or interest to know that the energy is being created due to your identification with your projection. What I mean by identification is that the possible negative outcome that you are projecting onto the future feels quite real to you. It feels like it could indeed happen. That means that it feels like it is a part of your reality, a part of your life and your experiences. It becomes part of your identity.

However, the understanding that you have become identified with your fear and the story that is generating it, that they feel like a real part of you, won't bring you back to the experience of *Pure Awareness*. You'll still be stuck inside the energy field of the emotion. In order to come out of its grip, you'll have to allow yourself to experience the entire energy field so that you can access the quietness out beyond the edge. This then experientially extracts your awareness from being collapsed inside the energy field and also extracts you from being identified with your projection.

What happens as you allow yourself to notice the background of silence in which the energy is occurring is that you begin to notice the vastness of *Pure Awareness*. It has no boundaries. It is limitless. And because *Pure Awareness* is the essential nature of what you truly are, when you experience it, the illusory nature of the story that you created, that became your projected possible negative outcome, no longer can maintain the appearance of being real. You are no longer collapsed inside of it. Because it can no longer maintain its appearance of being real, it simply starts to shrink back into the nothingness from which you created it. It is valuable to notice from a place of *Pure Awareness* that the fear that you were inside of was a fear generated by a story about something that hasn't happened. It's about something that doesn't actually exist in this moment. It may also be useful to notice that the story at the basis of the projection was something that you made up in your mind. It wasn't real. It didn't actually exist anywhere other than in your mind. The energy field that you created and that you had been living inside of is what made it seem so compellingly real.

It also may be valuable to simply notice that you were generating a huge field of energy in response to a story about something that has not yet occurred. Is the creation of stories like this and the fear associated with them really something useful to you? Is there any real value or benefit to doing this? Is this the way that you want to be using your life energy? Of course not!

When you have expanded your awareness to notice the quietness out beyond the outer edge of the energy field of the fear, you will find that the fear will simply fade away. And recognizing that the energy is a reaction to an unreal story will help you to let go of the conditioning that created this story in the first place.

You may find that it is initially easier to go through the SEE Technique with a guide. If that is the case, someone can easily read the script below and guide your through the SEE Technique. If you'd like to hear me explain the SEE Technique and guide some people through it, there is an audio recording available on the Internet at greatlifetechnologies.com/SEE-SANYAMA-GPS.html.

CHAPTER 13

How to Do the SEE Technique

Typically it is a good idea to find a quiet place where you won't be disturbed. Also make sure that you have a comfortable place to sit. It's better to do this sitting up rather than lying down. When you are first learning to do the SEE Technique, it is optimal to have someone guide you through the process by reading the instructions below to you. This can either be someone else who also wants to learn how to vaporize their anxiety or simply someone you trust, someone you know cares about you and will be sensitive and attentive to you as you learn this. Whether you choose someone who is going to learn the techniques with you with whom you will trade off reading and learning, or a spouse, a friend, or even if you hire a coach who has been trained to guide people through the *Pure Awareness* Techniques, make sure that it is someone with whom you feel comfortable and secure.

STEP 1 – READING YOUR LIST

The SEE Technique begins by reading your list of things that make you anxious. You will probably notice that many of them are ways in which you project some type of possible negative outcome onto the future. You certainly may not need to read the entire list. By simply reading some of the items that you put on the list you will probably be able to get in touch with things about which you are concerned, worried, or anxious. It might be a specific fear or it might be generalized fear of something uncertain or unknown. Just read the things that you have put on your list until you start to feel the anxious feeling. It might not take much. Remember that in order to resolve your anxiety that you are going to have to start by allowing yourself to feel the sensation of the anxious feeling in or around your body.

STEP 2 – FEEL THE ENERGY

Allow yourself to feel the energy of the emotion in and around your body. I know that this is exactly what you have not wanted to do. It's what you've been avoiding. But this is what has kept you dancing around the outer edges of the fear instead of resolving it. Let me assure you that the possibility of completely resolving the fear at the basis of your anxiety is right around the corner and that this isn't going to be as difficult as you think. It's actually going to be rather quick and easy. It is really only the child's perspective still held inside of us that causes us to not want to feel the energy of the fear. The way to get access to the energy of the fear is to think about an item from your list and simply decide to allow yourself to feel the energy of the fear about that thing. Once you can feel the energy of the fear in or around your body, then you will allow yourself to simply notice how big the energy field of the emotion is.

STEP 3 – READ THE SCRIPT

This is the point at which to have the person who has agreed to help you read the following script to you:

Note to the person reading the script to you

Read the parts in bold in "quotation marks" out loud. *Read the parts in the italics to yourself.* Allow the pauses to be long enough for the person doing the technique to absorb the instruction and maximize its use.

Start here -

"Notice that the emotion that you are feeling has a field of energy to it."

Pause (remember to pause long enough to allow them to be able to have the experience – if in doubt, continue the pause a little longer)

"Now allow yourself to notice that the field of energy radiates out from your body creating a cloud or aura of energy all around you."

Pause

"Simply allow yourself to notice how big the energy field of the emotion is. Sometimes the field can be pretty big."

Pause

"The way to do this is to allow your awareness, your attention, to expand outward from your body and notice whether or not the energy of the fear is still there or not. Keep letting your awareness expand more and more, checking if the energy of the fear is still there or not."

Pause

"As you continue to allow your awareness to expand, you will find that the field of energy of the fear has an outer limit to it. It may extend quite far beyond your physical body, but it doesn't go on forever. There is an outer edge of the energy field that might be very well defined or kind of vague. What we are looking for is the area where the energy fades away into quietness."

Pause

"Notice where the outer edge of the energy field of the emotion is, and that there is nothing else beyond it."

Pause

"Can you sense the quietness out beyond the outer edge of the energy field of the emotion?"

Pause - If they can't yet sense the quietness or they have not yet noticed the outer edge of the energy field, then say:

"Just keep allowing your awareness to expand more and more in order to notice the entire field of the energy until you find the outer edge and the quietness beyond it."

Pause

"Now take your awareness a little further beyond the outer edge of the emotion and notice that there is some quietness there."

Pause - Once they can sense the quietness out beyond the outer edge of the field of energy of the fear, then say:

"Notice the contrast between the energy field of the fear and the quietness that surrounds it."

Pause

"Now go even further from the outer edge of the fear, more deeply into the quietness that surrounds the field of its energy."

Pause

"Notice that this quietness surrounding the energy of the fear is much bigger than the energy field of the fear itself."

Pause

"Now notice that this quietness is actually a background of silence in which the energy field of the fear has been occurring."

Pause

"Notice that this background of silence doesn't

have any limits. Notice how, from the perspective of the vastness of the silent background, your story, the projection of some possible negative outcome onto the future, and the fear about that possibility, don't seem to have as much grip on you as they did before."

Pause

"Now just allow yourself to be in the vastness of the silent background, until there is nothing left of the energy of the emotion or the projection. It wasn't real to begin with. It doesn't exist in this moment. Enjoy the profound feeling of freedom that comes from experiencing that your projection and fear were just illusions."

Pause

"When the energy of the fear is completely gone, you can open your eyes."

Pause until the eyes are open and the person is back with you again.

After you have completed the SEE Technique, it is good to check to see if fear is completely resolved. You can do this by reviewing the issue that caused the initial reaction. Think about what it was and talk about it with your practice partner or reader. Notice if there is any energy, any charge of the fear left or not. If there is, you

may need to do the SEE Technique again, going out to
the outer edges and beyond the edges into the quietness
of *Pure Awareness*. Sometimes there may be several closely
related issues, each one of which has a layer of fear to it.
You can use the SEE Technique on the energy field of the
fear for each issue. When you check to see if there is any
energy of fear left after it has faded back into nothingness,
you will typically find that it is completely gone and you
have no inclination to bring it back. You might even
feel that having had the fear in the first place was kind
of ridiculous. The illusory nature of the story and the
associated fear become so obvious when looked at from
the state of *Pure Awareness* that one wonders why you
were ever afraid of something so unreal. The contrast is
sometimes so remarkable that it may at first seem too
good to be true. After all, how could something as visceral
and persistent as that old anxious feeling be completely
gone in just a few minutes? Even with this initial sense
of disbelief, many people laugh at the notion of ever
again creating such a ludicrous story and fear reaction.
However, if you find yourself harboring a fear that it
will come back, that fear is another candidate for using
the SEE Technique. Use the SEE Technique on any fears
that are still present and you will find that you quickly
liberate yourself from them. They are all inappropriate,
unreal fears of things that don't actually exist.

It is also good to know that sometimes there can be

one or more incomplete emotional experiences from the past that need to be resolved using the CORE Technique, which you will learn about next, after I give you some additional knowledge about the SEE Technique. Perhaps you had a terrifying experience in the past and not only did it leave an unresolved traumatic energy in your body but it also left you with the fear that something like that might happen again. If this is the case, you can switch back and forth from the SEE Technique to the CORE Technique and vice versa once you have learned them both. This is a very potent combination. I've yet to come across an emotional energy that could not be resolved using the SEE Technique, the CORE Technique, or a combination of both.

Why the SEE Technique Works So Well for Vaporizing Your Anxiety

[
The moment that you take your awareness out beyond the outer edge of the energy field of fear, in that moment you experientially extract yourself from identification with the story that is producing the energy.
]

ILLUSION VS. REALITY

The reason that the SEE Technique is so effective is because in the moment you take your awareness outside of the energy field of the fear, you liberate your awareness from being absorbed inside the illusion created by your projection that something might happen that you can't handle; *in short, it liberates you from your negative projections*. This is because when you bring your awareness out into the background of silence of awareness itself, you then have the direct experience of your essential nature, of your own awareness. The illusion that the story that you made up in your mind is real can't maintain the appearance of being real when directly experienced side by side with the reality of your own awareness. In the experiential comparison between reality and illusion, reality wins. Thus, the energy of the illusion of your story and the associated energy of the fear simply fade away into nothing.

CHAPTER 15

Using the SEE Technique to Breakthrough the Energy of Disassociation

A wonderful use of the SEE Technique is to help you come out of the experience of being disassociated from your feelings. This is especially useful for dealing with anxiety.

In a way, anxiety is a mild and fairly ineffective form of disassociation. We are trying to get away from the intensity of the energy of the fear, but we are stuck dancing around its edges. Often people suffering from anxiety are pretty good at being disassociated from their feelings. Sometimes they check out, numb out, or withdraw in order to avoid being overwhelmed by some intense experience. This is a natural survival response and it is entirely appropriate when it is needed. Going into a state of shock is an extreme example of this. It is the body's way of protecting itself.

However, sometimes the disassociation can last longer than necessary and you just feel disconnected from your feelings in general. The SEE Technique can work very well with this kind of disassociation. In this case, you need to allow yourself to feel the energy field of the disassociation. That might seem like a strange idea, but the disassociation does have an energy field to it and, actually, it will be quite familiar to you if you have been experiencing disassociation. When you use the SEE Technique on the disassociation energy, you may be surprised when you get to the outer edge of the energy field. I'll give you a couple of examples to make this clear.

I was teaching a seminar on the *Core Dynamics* and *Pure Awareness* Techniques in Germany in March of 2008. My host asked me if I would please work with a friend who was attending the seminar and use her for a demonstration in the class. He mentioned that she had had several traumas and needed some help. I was happy to do that.

As we started the session, the woman explained that she had experienced three sudden traumas in a span of just a few weeks. The first was that she was in an airplane that nearly crashed, but pulled up just at the last moment.

She certainly thought she was going to die. The second one was her father, with whom she was very close, died. The third one was that her cat that she had had for many, many years and loved dearly also died.

This woman explained that she could feel the pain of the loss of her cat and was very sad about that, but that she just couldn't feel any feelings about the near plane crash or about her father's death. She said that she knew that she must have some feelings about these events, but she couldn't access them. She was disassociated from these feelings.

We first used the CORE Technique to resolve the sadness about the loss of her cat, and within a few minutes the sadness was gone and she just felt her love for her cat.

Then we prepared to use the SEE Technique to resolve the energy of the disassociation. I asked her if she was prepared to feel the feelings that would be available when she let go of the disassociation. She said she was ready and willing to do that. So we started.

As soon as I asked her to go out to the outer edges of the disassociation energy field, she burst into tears. She had taken her awareness out to the outer edge of the energy of the disassociation very quickly and was then able to access the pain that the disassociation had previously been masking. Now she could feel the pain of the loss of her father. She cried for a little while, and when she settled down, I had her do the CORE Technique on the energy of the grief about her father. Again, within a short time she felt much better and the sadness was gone. She was also now able to access the residual terror feeling associated with the near crash of the airplane. We used the CORE Technique again for this traumatic energy of the terror. Finally, all of the energies of these traumas were completed and resolved. She was beaming and happy. She must have thanked me about ten times that day.

In another case, a man in Vancouver, Canada, who attended a presentation I gave, had been in a car accident several years before. He is the husband of one of my Master *Core Dynamics* Coaches. His wife asked if I could help him. He said that since the accident, he felt that he was living above and behind his body, looking down on himself. He was disassociated.

We did the SEE Technique on his energy of disassociation and, as he got to the outer edge of the energy field, he started laughing uncontrollably. After quite a long time of laughing he stopped, but shortly after started laughing again. When he finally settled down I asked him what he was experiencing. He said that coming out of the disassociation was such a huge relief that he couldn't help but laugh and laugh. He laughed again several times over the next half hour. He said that this was extraordinary because he couldn't recall the last time he had laughed at all. His wife was thrilled and he was happy.

The main thing to be aware of when using the SEE Technique on the energy of disassociation is that when you get to the outer edge of the energy field of the disassociation, there may be some surprise in store for you. Sometimes the energy of things that have been suppressed by the disassociation will burst forth because now you have access to them. It doesn't always happen but just be prepared to shift to using the CORE Technique or the SEE Technique again for the energy that's been hiding behind the disassociation, if needed.

Like the woman in Germany, you may need to experience crying or some other reaction for a bit before shifting to the CORE or SEE Technique. As you will learn in the section on the CORE Technique, we normally don't encourage crying, but rather we guide the person to go into the center of the energy that they are experiencing. However, sometimes when coming out of disassociation and being hit in the face, so to speak, with the full force of the suppressed emotions, there isn't any option but to allow the crying to happen. It will pass soon enough and you can then shift to the CORE or the SEE Technique as appropriate. If you don't know which one to use, just do one and if it doesn't work after a while switch to the other one.

CHAPTER 16

Remembering to Use the SEE Technique

As with all of the *Pure Awareness* Techniques, the key is remembering to actually do the technique. One good way to become proficient with the SEE Technique is to work with a Certified *Core Dynamics* Coach. All certified *Core Dynamics* Coaches are highly skilled at guiding you through all of the *Pure Awareness* Techniques. However, if you cannot access a professional coach, working with a trusted friend or colleague and utilizing the script will suffice. After being guided through the SEE Technique several times, you will naturally develop a sense of confidence in doing it on your own. You will also start to get a feel for the kinds of situations for which it is best used and helpful.

The SEE Technique can be used to defuse the energy of any fear with which you have become absorbed. For that matter it can be used to dismantle the energy of anything that really isn't you with which you have become identified. The key to success is to be able to get in touch with the energy of each emotion associated with each particular fear or identification.

The most common kinds of identifications, and the easiest ones to find, are the emotional energy of projections of possible negative outcomes onto the future and expectations that something will happen or not happen in a particular way. When you are identified with a projection of a possible negative outcome onto the future, the emotion will most likely be fear. If it is a projection of a possible negative outcome onto the future, all you need to do is think about the possibility of that negative outcome actually happening and you will very likely get in touch with the fear of that thing happening. That's when you start the SEE Technique and seek the outer edge of the energy field of the fear and the quietness out beyond its outer edges.

You can also use the SEE Technique to resolve the energy of other emotions as well. This is when the emotion is created in response to an unmet expectation. When you have an expectation, the emotion that you will feel if the expectation doesn't get met will already be present in you. It's as if there is a part of us that knows that the expectation isn't real, that it is a story that we have made up in our mind. And that part of us already has the seed of the emotional reaction there ready for us to experience the moment that the expectation isn't met. The emotional energy that is already present when you create the expectation will typically be disappointment, anger, frustration, sadness, etc.

Whatever the emotion, typically all you have to do to get in touch with it is to imagine the expectation not being met and you will be able to feel your latent reaction. Once you can feel the field of energy of the emotion, then use the SEE Technique to extract your awareness from its collapse inside the illusion that is creating this emotional energy. The emotional energy will fade away into nothing. Once it has faded away, it usually doesn't come back because you become so completely clear that it was just a story that you made up. It doesn't actually exist. The apparent reality of it will not seem real any more, and you'll be free of being stuck inside of this particular illusion.

Use the SEE Technique any time you feel caught in the grip of a negative emotion. If it doesn't seem to work, use the CORE Technique. With these two tools you can liberate yourself from the grip of any negative emotion.

CHAPTER 17

How Using the SEE Technique Impacts Your Life

The SEE Technique has an enormous potential to impact your life in ways that you have yet to imagine. Each time you do the SEE Technique, you are dismantling a piece of your illusory, false sense of self that is called your ego. As you continue to use it more and more you will find yourself recognizing when you are about to create an expectation or when you are starting to create a story projecting a possible negative outcome onto the future. And as you come to recognize what you are doing, you'll simply stop doing these things. The uselessness of expectations and projections and their associated emotional reactions will become increasingly obvious to you, to the point where you will simply stop creating these illusory stories.

This will increasingly free you to be fully present in the moment, rather than caught up in the illusions. When you are present, you are in *Pure Awareness*. In *Pure Awareness*, there is no ego, no fear, no anxiety; there is only the totality of your own awareness ready to respond to the needs of each moment with the fullness of your Being. This is a life worth living. It is living in the zone.

> When you are present, you are in Pure Awareness. In Pure Awareness, there is no ego, no fear, no anxiety; there is only the totality of your own awareness, ready to respond to the needs of each moment with the fullness of your Being. This is a life worth living.

You've probably had glimpses of this state of being when you are doing something that just flows effortlessly and it almost seems like *you* aren't even doing it. It happens in sports. It happens during creative projects. It can happen anytime. But what is truly wonderful is when it is the way that you experience life every moment of every day. It may sound unreal or fantastic to think that this could be a living reality, but this is only because your experiences of being in the zone have been rare. Living in the zone means living fully in the present, in the now.

By using the SEE Technique at every opportunity, you can rapidly dismantle your identifications, expectations, and projections that have kept you absorbed in the past and the future, so that you live life in the zone more and more, until it becomes your constant reality.

CHAPTER 18

Resolving Unresolved Fears From the Past— The CORE Technique

"I've been using the CORE Technique and it's just been amazing for me. Even when I've been anxious about things like money and bills I'm able to come out of the anxiety and fear so that I can just deal with everything so much better. It brings me back to a state of centeredness so that I can just do whatever needs to be done without staying caught up in the drama. I have thanked God every day for the CORE Technique. It is awesome and I am so grateful!

Barbara Whorley, Business Coach/Consultant/Speaker, Capo Beach, CA

Remember that there are two basic kinds of fear: projections of possible negative outcomes onto the future and incomplete, traumatic, fearful experiences from the past. You've just learned the SEE Technique for extracting yourself from the energy fields of fears that are created out of projections of possible negative outcomes onto the future. Now you're going to learn how to quickly and thoroughly resolve those traumatic fearful experiences from the past using the CORE Technique.

And you're going to be pleasantly surprised at how easy it is to do this.

I know that just considering having to face such traumas from the past seems like a daunting and unwanted task. But the person that you have become actually has the ability to resolve these kinds of experiences very easily and quickly. It's just that no one has ever showed you how to do that until now. If you feel anxious about learning to do this, first use the SEE Technique on that anxious feeling. You'll find that it is a projection of a possible negative outcome onto the future that's just a story in your mind. After you have resolved it, come back to this point in the book and you'll be able to tackle the CORE Technique with confidence.

You'll be using The CORE Technique to *Vaporize Your Anxiety* when the source of the anxiety is unresolved fears from the past. It is the best way I've found to heal from the unresolved childhood and other emotional traumas that are often at the root of your anxiety. Mastering this technique, which can be accomplished by simply practicing it often, will enable you not only to *Vaporize Your Anxiety*, but also to live in the richness of your emotional experiences without fear of being overwhelmed by them.

CORE is an acronym that stands for "Center of Remaining Energy." The energy of unresolved emotional experiences tends to undermine our adult lives. The key thing to keep in mind here is the insight that these emotional experiences are just patterns of energy.

The idea of dealing with this energy can seem daunting. We anticipate being uncomfortable, being brought back into the moment of the trauma that left it with us. But what is needed for the CORE Technique is to get in touch with the energy of the feeling that is still there in your body, not to become absorbed in reliving the memory of the circumstance that caused it in the first place.

The CORE Technique requires going inside to the center of the energy that's being held in different places in the body and experiencing it fully. This is the opposite of what we're conditioned to do. We're conditioned to move away from the energy, because of the Core Dynamic of *Resisting Feeling Things Fully* (see Part I, Chapter 5).

The problem with this, though, is that when you stay out at the edges, or even avoid allowing yourself to experience the energy of the incomplete experience at all, you're actually not avoiding it—you're holding onto it, tightly! As a result, it remains incomplete and becomes a barrier to so many things in life, especially when it comes to being clear about who you really are, what you want in life, and what you should do to achieve these things.

As I mentioned in the introduction, those of us who have anxiety don't handle stressful events very well. We often get caught up in fear and anxious feelings without seeming to have any control over the process. Minor things—a vague email from a coworker, a little pain somewhere in your body, a distressing local news story—can trigger an onset of anxiety. This can be very disconcerting, both because the anxiety itself is uncomfortable, and because you feel that it's inappropriate to have the reaction you're having.

But the thing to realize is, when something stressful or scary happens, it's usually not only the stress or scariness of the current situation that creates anxiety although that can certainly be the case. Often, the unresolved emotional pain from previous events is triggered by something stressful in the present, which then in turn triggers an attack of anxiety. Because the previous experiences were never completed, the energy associated with them is archived in the body, just waiting until a new experience triggers the old incompletion and brings it back into awareness. You end up feeling helpless and afraid. If certain circumstances trigger your anxiety, you can undoubtedly relate to what I'm talking about here.

However, when you begin to use the SEE and CORE

Techniques to *Vaporize Your Anxiety*, you are making two very conscious decisions. The first is to stop being the victim of your anxious feelings. You have the ability to master these feelings and move on. This may seem difficult at first but the more you do it, the easier it gets. Many people who have suffered from anxiety for a long time are highly identified with these feelings of being victimized, and with good reason. But now is the time to shed your skin of victimhood and move into the light of something new and wonderful.

The second decision you're making is to confront and resolve your emotions completely. Since anxiety is very uncomfortable, and in some cases even debilitating, my next statement may seem strange, but I assure you, my research and experience helping people resolve their anxiety bears it out: in most cases, anxiety is a *strategy* that allows people to avoid something else. In this case, that *something else* is simply some very intense emotional energy.

Imagine—at some subconscious level, you believe that anxiety is actually *better* than the alternative! The wonderful thing about the CORE Technique is that facing these pockets of intense, incomplete emotional energy in your body is not about dredging up painful memories or telling your most shameful stories to a therapist. It is simply about experiencing and completing the energy from the past that is still held in your body. When the energy is resolved the issue becomes a non-issue. This is a way to *Vaporize Your Anxiety* without spoiling your psychological state or having to relive old stressful events.

You will undoubtedly feel a lot when you begin to do the SEE and CORE Techniques. As you let go of anxiety, many suppressed emotions are likely to come into your awareness. Some of them may seem to show up with great intensity. It's important to be well prepared for this, or you may not stick with it until the energy of the feelings has been vaporized. But you've chosen to adopt a new strategy of healing—healing yourself from all the underlying fear and emotional pain. So hang in there—you can do it!

> In most cases anxiety is a strategy that allows people to avoid something else.

I feel that it is important to mention something here: If your anxiety seems to be there all the time, you may feel that it's just too much to tackle. Your mind may be racing so much that just calming down enough to do the CORE Technique seems beyond reach. I would like you to consider that the constant presence of this anxiety simply means that you have some fears that are so present and so unresolved that they are always with you. Even if this is the case, you will very likely be able to resolve them using the techniques you are learning in this book.

If, however, you try the CORE Technique, but feel as though your present-day fears are too omnipresent to cut through, I would like to encourage you to try the GAP Technique, which is described in Chapter 28, or the SEE Technique that you have already learned. I have found that for some people, the CORE Technique initially may seem a bit challenging. However, many of these people have wonderful success with the GAP or SEE Techniques, which allows them to quickly access a place of inner peace. Afterwards, using the CORE Technique to resolve older emotional pain tends to be much easier.

CHAPTER 19

Preparing to Learn the CORE Technique

[CORE – Center Of Remaining Energy]

As I've said, we tend to hold the patterns of incomplete experiences in our bodies. These incomplete experiences are made of energy, and the field of this energy typically feels rather like a hurricane. The intensity of the energy is stronger at the center and weaker at the edges.

Allowing yourself to go to the core, the most intense part of the energy of an incomplete emotional experience, is very exciting. It is sort of like sky diving right into the eye of a hurricane. As you move toward the center, it gets more and more intense, but when you arrive at the true center, you will suddenly encounter stillness.

You discover that it is actually safest and easiest to place your attention in the center of the most intense part of the energy of the feeling.

As it turns out, the way *OUT* of the anxiety and fear is actually . . . *IN*.

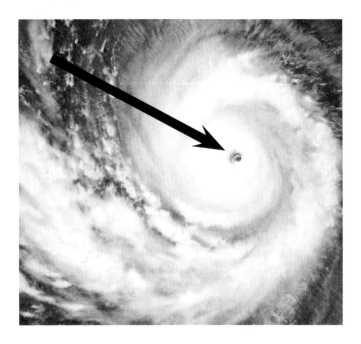

However, there are often layers of an incomplete emotional experience, each stacked on top of the others. As you dive down into the core of the energy, it seems to be gone, but then you find another layer of the incomplete experience. In fact, sometimes there can be several layers,

> Allowing yourself to go to the core – to the most intense part of the energy of an incomplete emotional experience – is exhilarating, sort of like sky diving right into the eye of a hurricane. The way OUT of anxiety and fear is actually… IN.

each with a different quality of feeling. That's just fine: when you encounter a new layer, you simply locate the core of the new layer and dive down into it.

This is not at all uncommon. In fact, I had this exact experience the first time I did the CORE Technique. I was having trouble in my marriage at the time. Something happened with my former wife that upset me and I was feeling angry. I don't remember what it was about (this is common, by the way, when the energy of an emotion is gone, the problem often seems unimportant anymore and is less memorable). However, I had promised myself that the next time I felt caught in the grip of an emotion like that, that I would try out this idea of feeling into the most intense part of the energy of the emotion. I remember clearly that there were layers to it because as I felt down into the anger so thoroughly that there wasn't any anger left, I found a feeling of hurt underneath it. Again I felt down into the energy of the feeling of hurt until there was nothing left to feel. Under that there was deep sadness. And beyond that, a feeling of being alone and isolated. But when I had felt into the most intense part of each of these layers of unresolved feelings, they finally were all resolved and there was nothing left of any of them. It was like the clouds burning off in the morning sun. Everything just opened up and expanded, and I was in a clear experience of *Pure Awareness*.

It is not uncommon to have emotions stacked one on top of the other like this. If you happen to have this experience, that there are layers of feelings stacked on top of each other, just find the center of each one in turn and feel down into them until there is nothing left to feel.

Another thing to be aware of is that sometimes the layers of an incomplete emotional experience have been stored in several different places on *your internal hard drive* (your body). You may find that when the energy of one layer seems to be fading away, the energy of another layer will start to be experienced in another part of your body. Again, this is completely normal. Whether there are several layers or just one, and whether the layers are in one location or in several, when you feel your way down into the core of the most intense part of the energy you will eventually find… nothing. And this, believe it or not, is really what we're after: the "nothingness" out of which we create all of our experiences—even the reactions to our emotions that we're now getting rid of.

Interestingly, this nothingness from which the energy

of the reaction was created corresponds very well to what is called the "Unified Field" in quantum physics. Unified Field theory holds that various forces are really manifestations of one larger unifying principle. So when you complete the experience of the energy of the reaction that's been stored, you are directly experiencing the quantum field from which the energy of the experience had manifested.

CHAPTER 20

Practice: Using the CORE Technique to *Vaporize Your Anxiety*

Again before you begin, find a quiet place where you can have some privacy. Also find a comfortable chair. Once you make yourself comfortable, you are ready to begin. You know what the CORE Technique is. You've made your list of anxiety-triggering situations, being as specific as possible.

To do the exercise below, I recommend that you find someone you're comfortable with and go through the exercise with this person guiding you. The best person for this is a close friend or a spouse, someone you trust and who is willing to be there for you without judgment, just to help. Or it can also be someone who wants to learn the *Pure Awareness* Technique too, a practice partner. Practicing the CORE Technique with someone guiding you through it the first few times will make it easier to learn than simply attempting to do it yourself.

As you read your list of anxiety-producing topics, you'll find that one or more of them will stand out as the easiest to use to access the energy of the anxious feeling in or around your body. It is sometimes difficult to pinpoint the location in your body where you experience the physical sensation of anxiety. That's OK. Anxious feelings often can feel like they're *everywhere*, or *enveloping* your body. You may even feel like you're being consumed by the energy. Usually when this is the case it is best to start with the SEE Technique and just see how big the field of energy is. Then go beyond the outer edge of the energy field into *Pure Awareness* and let the energy fade away. If after doing the SEE Technique there is still some energy held in the body, it will usually be easier to locate and also easier to feel after having first done the SEE Technique.

The SEE Technique will be helpful when you are having a hard time finding the place in your body where the energy of the anxiety is held because you don't need to find it. You can simply start with the cloud of energy that you feel all around you.

Normally, when practicing the CORE Technique, the very first question is something along the lines of *"Where do you feel the energy in your body?"* But after working with many people who suffer from anxiety, I began to realize that this was often not easy to locate. So if this is the case for you, start with the SEE Technique and see if afterwards you still need the CORE Technique.

To start off, we have to bring your attention to the field of energy of the anxiety. This alone can be challenging, because it means that you have to allow yourself to feel the anxious feeling. You may have anxious feelings all the time or you may only feel anxious under certain circumstances. If you feel anxious all the time, it shouldn't take much to notice the feeling of anxiety. If you only get anxious about certain things, it should still be pretty easy to get in touch with feeling anxious. Just use your list and allow yourself to think about one of the situations or circumstances that make you anxious. Whether you feel anxious all the time or just under certain circumstances the idea is to start by simply allowing yourself to feel the entire feeling of the anxious energy.

And remember this:

> With the SEE Technique, you moved outward, beyond the outer edge of the anxiety. With the CORE Technique you are moving inward until you reach the eye of the storm of your anxiety.

Have your practice partner read the following instructions before starting to read the script to you:

Read the bold sections in quotation marks (" ") out loud *and read the italicized sections silently to yourself.* Remember that when there is a pause you need to pause long enough to allow the person to have a good clear experience of what you have just asked them to do. The length of the pause may vary according to the instruction. You can just use your intuition to guide you as to how long to pause before reading the next instruction.

Start here

"Please sit comfortably and close your eyes."

Wait for a few moments, then say:

"Allow yourself to feel the entire feeling of the field of the energy of the anxiety. Just let yourself be fully present and feel the whole of its energy."

Pause here for a moment before continuing.

"You may start to gradually notice that in the field of energy there is an area where it is more concentrated, more condensed."

Pause

"It will usually tend to be toward the center of the body somewhere, in your chest, solar plexus, or belly, but it could be anywhere."

Pause

"It may take a little while of allowing yourself to feel the entire field of the energy of the anxious

feeling before you will begin to notice this more condensed area within the field of the energy, so just take your time."

Pause

"When you do notice the area that is more condensed somewhere towards the center of your body you can let me know by just nodding or say OK."

(Pause and let them be with the experience. When they either nod or say OK you can continue reading.)

"Now that you can feel the area of the energy that is more concentrated or condensed, where in your body do you feel it?"

They will say where they feel it or gesture to an area in the chest or stomach or throat or somewhere. Then say:

"If you allow yourself to, you can sense in that field of energy that there is an area where it is even more intense than it is elsewhere. Can you sense that?"

They will typically acknowledge this with a nod or a yes. If not you can tell them to just allow themselves to feel the field of the energy for a little while and see if after a time they notice that there is an area that is more intense than elsewhere. In a short time they will tend to say yes. At that point, say:

"Now allow yourself to let your awareness go right into the center of the most intense part of the energy of the sensation."

Pause

"Can you do that?"

Pause—(get acknowledgment)

"Okay, go ahead and continue."

Now. . . WAIT until you have a sense that it's appropriate to speak again. This will range from less than a minute to a minute or two or even more. Then slowly and gently say:

"Usually one of three things happens. Sometimes the sensation will become more intense at first as you haven't been allowing yourself to feel it fully. Sometimes it will seem to stay the same for a time. And sometimes it may start to fade away or soften. Is one of these things happening?"

Typically they will nod or say yes. If they don't volunteer anything you can ask:

"Which one of these are you experiencing?"

There are three possible responses -

1. It's getting more intense.

2. It seems to be staying the same.

3. It seems to be fading away or becoming softer less intense.

For either #1 or #2 you can then say:

"OK, simply continue to allow your awareness to feel right into the center of the most intense part of the energy of the sensation."

Then give them some time to do that.

For #3—fading away/becoming softer or less intense—say:

"Now bring your awareness in closer to whatever is left of the sensation, again find the center of intensity of the remaining energy, and again allow yourself to feel down into it, just experiencing the essence of the energy."

"The idea is to feel down into the energy of the sensation so thoroughly that there is nothing left to feel."

Give them some time to do this. Then check in again with them to see what is happening. You can say:

"How's it going?"

They may have had some visual experience or the energy they are sensing may have moved to a different place. They may have completed the experience and the energy will have dissipated, and there's nothing left. If they say anything other than that what they found in there was nothing, you have to continue to guide them into the core of the energy of the experience.

"Is there any of the sensation of the energy left"

Or:

"Is there any charge left?"

If they say yes, say:

"Okay, I'd like you to again place your awareness into the center of the most intense part of whatever is left of that energy. We're not looking for insights, just experiencing the energy of an incomplete experience. This is just the process of completing the experience of the energy that has been held in your body. I'd like you to allow yourself to experience it so thoroughly that there is nothing left to experience."

Continue with them in this way. In the vast majority of cases, the person will come out of the grip of the energy of the incomplete experience, and they'll say something like, "It's better," or "It's gone," or "There's nothing there."

Once they realize that there is nothing left and there is no more energy of the sensation, you can now do what is called a "provocation test." This is to make sure that they really fully experienced every bit of the energy of the incomplete emotional experience and there's truly nothing left of it. Say to them:

"Now that it appears to be gone we are going to check to see that it's really complete. So I'd like you to think about the original thing that was causing you to feel anxious."

Give them a moment. Then say:

"Do you still feel anxious?"

If they should say, "Yes, I still feel anxious." there are two possibilities,

1. Ask if this is the same anxious feeling as the one that they started with. It may be that there is more than one anxious feeling and even if one of them has been resolved using the CORE Technique they may now be feeling another one. If this is the case making this distinction may help the person to appreciate that the technique has worked for resolving ONE of their anxious energy patterns. They may want to continue to use either the CORE or SEE Technique for resolving the additional anxious feeling now or at a later time.

2. It may feel like there is still a residue of the initial anxious feeling. If this is the case they may simply need to click in closer again and feel into the remaining energy of the incomplete experience until there really is nothing left to feel. You can again say:

"Okay, I'd like you to again place your awareness into the center of the most intense part of whatever is left of that energy. We're not looking for insights, just experiencing the energy of an incomplete experience. This is just the process of completing the experience of the energy that has been held in your body. I'd like you to allow yourself to experience it so thoroughly that there is nothing left to experience."

However, typically when you have taken them back into the center of the energy and had them feel into it until there is nothing left to feel, they'll say "No. It's gone." (Don't be surprised if they smile or look relieved.) Then you can say this:

"You are no longer limited by the presence of the energy of that was causing these anxious feelings. Your body has been trying to get you to fully feel this energy and complete the experience that was held there. Now it is complete and your body has stopped creating this energy."

"There was an experience of something there that your body needed you to get, not intellectually but experientially. From this place that you're in now, this place of nothingness, you have total freedom of choice. You're in a state of all possibilities where anxiety doesn't exist."

They may have opened their eyes by now, but if they haven't you can invite them to do that now. This is the end of the guidelines for doing the CORE Technique.

———————————————

You can continue reading the book by yourself now.

Whether you're someone who has been feeling anxious more or less all the time, or just under certain situations, check to see if that old familiar anxious feeling is still there or not. I'll bet it's gone. This process of thinking about the anxiety or the circumstances under which you feel anxious is called a *provocation test*. It is designed to help you make sure that you really completed the experience of the energy of that feeling. Sometimes you might still feel something when you think of it again. If you do, just go back inside and bring your awareness in close to any remaining energy that might still be there. Feel into the core of it so that you complete the experience of whatever is left of it. If it continues to feel like there is still some energy there, use the SEE Technique to see how big it is and go out beyond its outer edge into the quietness of *Pure Awareness*. I have yet to find an emotional energy that cannot be resolved by the SEE or the CORE Technique, or toggling back and forth between them.

If it doesn't seem like an emotion, feel into the most intense part of whatever it is such as the sense of emptiness

PATTERNS OF ENERGY YOU MAY NOT RECOGNIZE AT FIRST

The question of *Pure Awareness* brings up another point I'd like to make. Sometimes when you feel into something, it may not be obvious at first that what you are feeling is a pattern of energy. This is especially true for things like *feeling empty*. Emptiness doesn't seem like it would be a feeling or a pattern of energy. The trick to being able to catch these patterns of energy that don't seem like they could be patterns of energy—and certainly don't seem like *feelings*—is to use the very nature of what they *feel like* as the way to get at them.

In other words, if you are feeling empty, allow your awareness to go to the area that feels the *MOST* empty. This is a version of feeling into the most intense part of the energy of the feeling. There is a subtle but important difference between the *feeling of emptiness* and the experience of the nothingness of *Pure Awareness*. When we use the phrase *a feeling of emptiness*, there is an implied expectation that something should be there, that something is missing. This is in contrast to the experience of *Pure Awareness*, in which, even though there is no object of experience, the sense of *no-thingness* feels alive and vibrant, and there is a sense of limitless potential, a feeling of pure possibility. Whereas emptiness is the experience of feeling the lack of something, *Pure Awareness* is the true source of all of our experiences. In *Pure Awareness* there is no sense of lack. So if you feel *empty,* try simply feeling into the most intense part of the emptiness, the place where it feels the emptiest and notice how very different emptiness is from *Pure Awareness*. Alternately, use the SEE Technique and see how big the field of the energy of the emptiness is. You'll find that it has an outer limit to it and that beyond it is that lively quietness of your own awareness.

This brings up another important point about both the SEE and the CORE Techniques. There may be a tendency to expect the feelings that come up to be the same every time you use these techniques. Although they may sometimes be similar, the quality of the experience of the energy is often absolutely unique, as with the case of the *feeling* of emptiness. The way in

> Whereas emptiness is an experience of lack, Pure Awareness is an experience of abundance.

which the energy goes away may also be different. So it is optimal just not to have any expectation of exactly what the experience is going to be like.

[
If it's bothering you, if it's making you uncomfortable, and especially if you don't want to feel it, that's the perfect indication that it needs to be felt and completed.
]

There may be other feelings that surprise you—because you wouldn't typically characterize them as feelings. So it may be good to simply think of them as any experience other than *Pure Awareness*. Once you have done the SEE and the CORE Technique many times you will become quite familiar with *Pure Awareness*. You'll be able to tell when something you are experiencing is *NOT Pure Awareness*. If it's bothering you, if it's making you uncomfortable, and especially if you don't want to feel it, that's the perfect indication that it needs to be felt and completed.

CHAPTER 21

When to use the CORE Technique

You can use the CORE Technique any time you feel like you are getting anxious, or for that matter, anytime you feel like you are becoming lost to the grip of emotion. However for anxiety, as I have mentioned previously, it is usually best to start with the SEE Technique and then switch to the CORE Technique as a second step if the energy doesn't completely go away.

Sometimes a circumstance will trigger the incomplete experience of some fear from the past and you may feel anxious again or you may feel some other uncomfortable feeling. This is the perfect time to remember to use the CORE Technique. Once you are released from the grip of the emotion, you have reached the state of *Pure Awareness*, a state from which you can make the best decisions for your life. Use the SEE Technique and then the CORE Technique, if needed, every time you feel that your anxiety or your emotional reactions are getting the better of you, and you will never have to be the victim of anxiety or other emotions again.

You can use the CORE Technique in two different ways:

1. **Use it on your own to resolve any feelings of anxiety that come up.** You can use it to come away from the grip of emotion when you feel you are becoming overwhelmed, or when you just have some feeling you would like to resolve. When this happens, it's just an indication that there is something present that you don't want to feel. It's a big red flag that can be a helpful reminder that it's time to simply scan your body, find the discomfort that you do not want to feel, and instead, use the CORE Technique. You can use the preliminary step, which asks you to feel the entire field of the energy of the anxiety if you can't initially find the center of it. By feeling the entire field of the energy of the anxiety you'll gradually become aware of the area that is more concentrated, more intense. Make sure to feel the essence of the energy of the feeling so thoroughly that there is nothing left to feel.

2. **Use it in the context of *Core Dynamics* Coaching sessions**. A trained *Core Dynamics* Coach will ask you questions to help you identify any "archived" incomplete emotional energy that

could also be a source of anxiety. *Core Dynamics* Coaches are trained to skillfully inquire about the nature of what is happening inside of you. They are able to gently get you in touch with anything that could be a potential cause of anxiety. They will then carefully guide you through the CORE Technique to resolve the basis of your fear and help you to vaporize it.

A few words of additional guidance here may be helpful. Because you are deeply conditioned to want to move away from where the emotional energy is the most intense, you will have an automatic tendency to not use the CORE Technique. It's much more familiar to just stay stuck in the anxiety. This is why it is good to have someone guide you through the process by reading the script to you in the beginning. It is important to go through the process of using the CORE Technique several times when you are learning it so that you learn to use it instead of collapsing back into old anxious patterns. A practice partner will help you stay on track. This leads us to the next important point.

A COMMON MISTAKE TO WATCH OUT FOR

The biggest mistake you can make with the CORE Technique is not to *complete* the experience of the energy that is being held in your body. Sometimes, especially when people are first learning how to do the CORE Technique, they will feel into the feeling for a while and will then back away from it before it is complete. Instead of completing the experience they will open their eyes and say, *"It's better."* What you need to recognize is that this is the result of the same preverbal conditioning—the Core Dynamic of Resisting Feeling Things Fully—that caused you to want to get away from the feelings in the first place! After an initial lessening of intensity, many people who are new to the CORE Technique feel like they want to stop and not feel it any more under these circumstances. So be on the lookout for this pitfall—it is very important to understand the dynamic that's at work here, and to keep feeling deeper into the center of the sensation, until there is literally nothing left to feel.

The most important thing to do is to make sure that you complete the experience of the energy of the emotion. The concept to remember is this:

[Feel into the core of the energy of the feeling so thoroughly that there is nothing left to feel.]

CHAPTER 22

Doing the
MapQuest Thing

> As the energy starts to fade away click in closer—bring your awareness in closer to whatever remains of the energy and feel down into it until there is nothing left to feel.

Something that can help to ensure that you *do* feel into the core of the energy until there is nothing left to feel is what we've started calling *doing the MapQuest thing*. When you're using MapQuest or any other mapping program on the internet and you want to get a closer view, you *click in*, meaning that you click the map, and then zoom in which brings you closer so you see a greater level of detail. It is like increasing the magnification using a telescope or a telephoto lens from an airplane or satellite.

When you are feeling into the core of a feeling and it starts to fade away, rather than succumbing to the tendency to call it a day and stop feeling into it, you can *click in closer*, bringing your awareness closer to whatever remains of the energy of the sensation. Again, find the center of the remaining energy and continue to feel down into it. The idea is to keep feeling into the core, then click in closer, feel into the core again, click in closer again, and just keep repeating this process until there is literally nothing left to feel.

Another issue is related to the attitude toward the emotions held in your body. Due to the conditioning of Resisting Feeling Things Fully, we typically strive to *make the bad feeling go away!* This is simply because we're afraid of being overwhelmed by the feeling. We've had an entire lifetime of perpetu-

ating the childhood notion that we can't handle the feeling and are going to be overwhelmed by it.

This can cause us to try to move too quickly—to *force* the completion of experiencing the energy of the feeling. But you must understand that the CORE Technique is not about *making the feeling go away* or *getting rid of the feeling*. It is about having a truly complete experience of the energy of the feelings in your body. Forcing the process will tend to cause straining and resistance, which can actually get in the way of allowing yourself to truly complete the experience of the energy.

It took me years to realize this simple idea, but now I understand that when there is incomplete emotional energy stored in the body, there is simply some experience our body is trying to get us to complete. The attitude of *getting rid of it* tends to cause us to stuff or repress the feeling. This ignores the body's innate intelligence, which is trying to offer us what I call *experiential wisdom*. The completion of the experience of truly feeling the energy of an emotion in the body grants us the experiential wisdom that enables the body to stop needing to create that energy, once and for all.

Remember, the CORE Technique is all about gaining the skill of completing incomplete experiences. So it is really important to shift your attitude from one of *making it go away* to one that will allow you to simply feel the energy until there's nothing left to feel.

[The CORE Technique is all about
gaining the skill of completing
incomplete experiences.]

LASER-LIKE FOCUS

Sometimes during the process of practicing the **CORE** Technique it can seem like it's taking a long time to complete the experience you're having of the intense energy of a backlogged emotional experience. When this happens, it is often the expression of some of the subtle influences of the Core Dynamic of *Resisting Feeling Things Fully*. If you are in the habit of moving away from where the energy of the sensation is most intense, your awareness may tend to spread out—kind of like a flashlight beam. If your

[Make your awareness
like a laser-beam
going right down the
center of the most
intense part of the
energy]

awareness is more like a flashlight beam, you will tend not to complete the experience of the energy of the feeling very quickly. Although we aren't in a rush when we're doing the CORE Technique, we do want to be efficient about completing the experience.

If you feel like the focus of your awareness on the center of the feeling is too spread out, try this simple exercise:

As you move to the center of the energy of the feeling, imagine that your awareness is a super-fine laser beam. Allow the laser beam to go right into the very center—the most intense part—of the energy. This simple process can make a big difference in how long it takes to complete the experience of the energy that is held there. Because the CORE Technique is all about finding the most concentrated part of the energy of the feeling, you may find that this will complete the experience of the energy more efficiently.

This is not to say that one couldn't resolve these experiences with a flashlight beam. But as I mentioned before, we want to be as efficient as possible. This is not, as with some forms of therapy, about spending a lot of time re-experiencing things. We want to only spend as much time as is actually necessary to fully experience the energy of our old stored emotions, and then move on. When we use a laser-like focus of our awareness, it can make the difference between spending moments in the process, and spending hours or even days to complete it. Like learning a musical instrument, you'll find that you become more skilled with practice. Each time you do the technique you'll get better and better at it. After doing the CORE Technique a couple of dozen times, you'll discover to your delight that you can feel down into the energy of a feeling with laser-like precision, and the process will be completed sometimes literally in seconds.

CHAPTER 23

Subtle Variations of the CORE Technique

Now I'll tell you about some of the different kinds of experiences you may have with the CORE Technique, and give you some of its refinements and subtleties. There is a wide range of possible experiences using the CORE Technique, and as you do it more often, you may experience some of them. We have found that having a little preview of some of the kinds of experiences that can occur can be helpful, so that you will not resist your natural experiences or become concerned if any of these things show up.

THE EYE OF THE HURRICANE

As explained earlier, sometimes as you feel down into the energy of the sensation or feeling in the body, it will seem as if there is a vortex, a kind of hurricane's eye, right in the center of the energy. If you experience this, let your awareness be like a laser beam going right down the center of the vortex. Keep following it down until you *come out the bottom*, and it will open up into the experience of *Pure Awareness*.

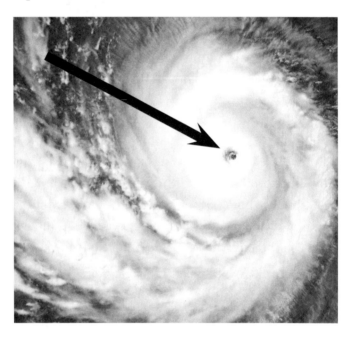

WHAT IF I FEEL LIKE CRYING?

Sometimes you may feel the energy is just too intense, and you may feel inclined to let yourself be sucked into it or overwhelmed by it. You may feel like you are about to cry. There's nothing wrong with crying, but it may not be the most efficient way to completely resolve the

> If you feel like crying, go right into the center of the intensity. Don't bounce off the walls, don't collapse into the energy of crying.

energy of the incomplete emotion that is held there. If you think about it for a moment, at what age did you learn to be overwhelmed by emotions and collapse into the feeling and cry? Pretty young, that's for sure! Allowing yourself to collapse into crying and be overwhelmed by the energy of an emotion is a learned behavior from a time when your capacity to feel things was much smaller than it is now. You were very young and had a delicate nervous system that was easily overwhelmed. You developed the habit of crying at that time because it was all you could do.

Certainly there is some release from the emotion that happens from crying, but often there will still be residual energy there that can be triggered again by certain circumstances. Crying then becomes yet another way to avoid feeling into the core of the energy. I understand that this may seem counterintuitive. After all, we live in an age that is finally making it more acceptable to feel things and show our emotions. I certainly don't want to discourage anyone from the very natural experience of crying, when it is appropriate. But my experience has shown that to achieve our true aim—resolving these incomplete experiences that are being held in the body so thoroughly and completely that they no longer are a barrier to our experiencing *Pure Awareness* all the time—crying can actually be a hindrance. You see, as long as we continue to avoid feeling these incomplete feelings held in the body, they act as a kind of screen between us a natural state of inner peace, and they tend to keep us in a state of anxiety.

I have consistently found that instead of crying, it is usually much more helpful to take one's awareness to the center of the intensity of the incomplete emotional energy and feel down into it until the experience is complete. This will free you from any residual energy that the body is trying to get you to feel. The body is very tenacious. It will keep producing the same energy until you allow yourself to complete that experience. Once it is complete you are free of it forever.

It's like running anti-virus software on yourself. Once the virus is gone, it's gone and won't come back unless the computer is re-infected, unless you have another traumatic experience similar to the previous one that put it there. But there is very little likelihood that this will happen, because you are much stronger now. You know how to do the CORE Technique, which will help prevent already-completed energy from ever coming back.

Even if you do have another overwhelming experience

that is similar to the one you completed, you have the CORE Technique that you can use to complete any new or similar incompletion you may encounter. You're already good at this, so there's no problem! More importantly, as you practice the CORE Technique over time, you will gain the skill of staying present for intense emotional experiences without being overwhelmed. You'll be able to experience emotional intensity much more easily because you will have been exercising and expanding your capacity to feel. And when you fully experience things in the moment, as they happen, your body doesn't have to store the incomplete emotional energy for later processing. Think of the freedom you'll experience!

CHAPTER 24

Remembering to Use the CORE Technique

"Almost every time I notice a reaction to something emotional or mental, I have learned to find the area where I feel it, embrace it, and then watch and feel it dissolve. It is amazing the changes it has made in my life. I now find that the moment I feel a reaction, I do the CORE Technique, usually in seconds. Those things that used to bother me don't have a charge, or much charge, anymore."

—Elizabeth Witcofski, Phoenix, AZ

> The most important aspect of the CORE Technique is remembering to use it.

As with any new skill, like meditation or learning to play an instrument, the most important thing is simply to practice. So the most important thing about the CORE Technique is… remembering to use it! Once you have learned it and put it to use, you've upgraded your inner human software. It is as if you now have a new icon for an "inner human software" program sitting on your "inner desktop." Just like with computer software, though, this new upgraded software isn't going to do you much good unless you double click on it and use it! In other words, don't just *learn* the techniques in this book like a subject in school. There's no exam at the end of the book! Instead of learning them, *use them*. Incorporate them into your daily life so that if you find you are caught in the grip of anxiety and fear—or for that matter, any strong, negative emotion you experience—you don't have to stay stuck there.

The best way to remember to use this wonderful new tool is to make a *decision* that you are going to become really good at it and that you are going to use it every time you feel anxious or worried. As Anthony Robbins said in *Awaken the Giant Within*, "I believe that it's in your moments of *decision* that your destiny is shaped."[9] If you make a real decision to bring the CORE Technique into your life, you will follow through effortlessly. After you have done the CORE Technique a couple of dozen times you will have probably overcome your reticence about feeling your feelings so fully. Then the CORE Technique will simply become a normal part of your skill set, like reading silently. You won't have to try hard to remember to use it because it will have become a natural

---

9 Robbins, Anthony. Awaken the Giant Within. Free Press, New York. 1991. pp. 32-33.

part of your life. It will be right there and you'll use it whenever the need arises.

One of your challenges will be that you are already very used to having anxiety. It's familiar to you. And you may have had it so long that it seems normal. So one tricky issue is going to be recognizing that you are in an anxious state and then remembering to do this special application of the CORE Technique to vaporize the underlying fear that is at the basis of your anxiety.

Another issue is in trying new things. As we discussed earlier, most of us don't like change. We may even fear it. For some, embracing change, embracing something new, is like stepping into the cold ocean. It causes trepidation, even its own anxiety. But once we jump in, the water usually seems to warm up, and by the time we get out, we are glad to have had the experience. It is the same with doing these Techniques.

The best part is that you don't even need to know what it is that you are anxious about! And you don't need to know what the deeper fear at the basis of your anxious feelings is either. You might get an insight sometimes as to what the deeper cause of the anxiety is, but it really doesn't matter. Intellectually knowing what it is rarely makes the fear go away, as you may already know very well. What's needed is to vaporize the underlying fear experientially. Then the experience of the energy of the fear gets completed and the anxiety disappears.

All you have to do is to find somewhere you can sit quietly, close your eyes, and scan your body. First you will probably find some generalized anxiety feelings or you might have a feeling of getting panicky. As you allow yourself to feel the whole field of the anxious feeling you will usually start to feel some tightness or ache or emptiness or some kind of feeling somewhere in your body. When you find it, use the CORE Technique to feel down into it completely until there is nothing left to feel. When you are done you can check to see if there's any anxiety left and you will often find that it is gone. If it isn't, that means there's something else to feel. Scan your body again and feel into and complete anything that your body is calling out to you to feel. If it still isn't completed, use the SEE Technique. Between the CORE and the SEE techniques, anxiety doesn't stand a chance of continuing to spoil your life!

When you have completed even one of the fears that has been causing your anxiety, you will feel a renewed sense of peace and silence inside. The anxiety will be gone because you have completed the experience of the underlying fear that you had been avoiding by staying out at the edges of the field of energy of the feeling. Once you have this experience a few times you'll be able to remember to use the CORE Technique whenever you need it.

CHAPTER 25

EEG Validation of the CORE Technique

In January of 2007, I attended a conference on neuro-feedback in Palm Springs, CA called *The Winter Brain Meeting*. During the conference I had the opportunity to test a new form of EEG monitoring equipment to be able to see the brain wave indications of deep emotional releases that people get using the CORE Technique and other techniques that produce inner calm.

Great Life Technologies had a booth at the conference and I was mainly there to share our recent successes with debugging the underlying causes of ADD and ADHD using **Human Software Engineering**. I gave a presentation about our work with this new approach. I also had the opportunity to give numerous demonstrations. People were interested, and many practitioners, heads of large clinics, and neuro-feedback device manufacturers inquired about **Human Software Engineering**.

I began to explain the *Core Dynamics* of Common Problems to a woman at the conference who was fascinated with our work and wanted to know more. As we talked, she shared that the past year had been difficult for her, and that she was feeling stressed and very anxious as a result. She was a mid-level executive at a large company and had been considering a change of career. She had never experienced anxiety before this period, which in itself was probably contributing greatly to her anxiety. (By the way, this is a very common situation for people who have an onset of anxiety later in life).

I helped her to identify where in her body she was holding the energy of all of this stress. It turned out to be in her solar plexus, which was very interesting. In the Eastern religious traditions, the site of the 3rd chakra is the solar plexus. Sometimes called *The Power Chakra*, it is associated with will power, vitality, and personal power. According to Eastern tradition, when people are out of balance in this chakra, they will experience feelings of powerlessness: fear of taking risks, fear of confronting people or issues, fear of taking charge. In other words, they are stuck *dancing at the outer edges of fear*, and they commonly experience what we call *anxiety*.

Using one of the advanced *Core Dynamics* coaching techniques, I debugged her inner human software for the Core Dynamic of *Resisting Feeling Things Fully*, and I explained the nature of the kind of preverbal, precognitive conditioning that produces our inner resistance to self-healing this kind of stress. I was just starting to teach her the CORE Technique and thought to ask her if she'd like to do this while using the new iCAP EEG monitoring device. This would allow us to see the effect of the technique on her brain waves. She replied affirmatively, so we went to the iCAP booth that was right next to the Great Life Technologies booth and asked if we could use it. The iCAP folks were very enthusiastic about it, especially since it was so simple to put on the headband, turn the unit on and start the software on the laptop.

As I guided her into the CORE of the feeling I got to watch what was happening with the EEG on the monitor. With the iCAP system, a drop in the indicator line means that there is a release of stress and/or emotional energy occurring. At a certain point, about three and a half minutes into the session, and after a short instruction about allowing herself to go right into the center of the most intense part of the energy of the feeling, there was a dramatic drop in the EEG indicator line.

Right at that moment, one of the founders of the iCAP company who was sitting nearby happened to look over. When he saw what was happening on the monitor, his eyes widened and his jaw dropped open! He waited for a few moments. He could see that she was in the middle of a huge release. Then he said quietly (but with a strong enthusiasm in his voice), *Wow, your stuff really works! Getting below 300 is really extraordinary!* In fact, the reading from the EEG had gone down into the 270's range during that big drop.

Here's what it looked like on the screen (with my notations added). The dashed line is the signal from the first 3 minutes of the exercise. The solid line shows the activity of the second three minutes. She was starting to get the hang of it toward the end of the dashed line, then even more during the first 30 seconds of the solid line. At about 45 seconds into the solid line portion of the session she completely let go of the big knot of stress that she had been holding onto. Later she said that it was the cumulative stress of the entire past year and that she felt transformed during these few minutes.

EEG BRAIN SCAN DURING A SESSION USING THE
CORE TECHNIQUE

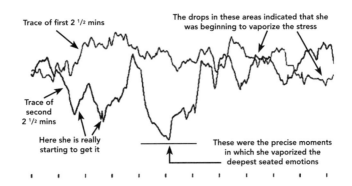

It was great to meet the people from the iCAP company and learn about their new EEG technology. It's a unique new form of EEG monitoring that is specifically designed to pick up and display brain wave patterns that indicate deep emotional releases. Best of all, it's very user friendly—it's completely wireless, and it doesn't even require moisture for the sensor that picks up the brain waves. The small sensing unit is mounted in a simple headband and sends a wireless signal to a small USB receiving device that brings the data into a very simple interface on your computer. The software allows you to witness in real time the direct effect of doing techniques that release emotions and create a deep state of relaxation. And in addition to monitoring the emotional releases that occur in the moment, it can track your progress in cleaning out your emotional baggage over time. See my article at www.greatlifetechnologies.com/ICAP.shtml for more information about the iCAP.

CHAPTER 26

Scientific Research on the Use of the *Pure Awareness* Techniques for Reducing Anxiety

As of this writing, a scientific study on the use of the *Pure Awareness* Techniques for reducing anxiety symptoms is underway at the Laboratory for the Study of Anxiety Disorders at the University of Texas–Austin, under the direction of the founder of this organization, Dr. Michael Telch. Dr. Telch has been studying anxiety disorders for over 25 years and is an internationally recognized expert in this field. The study began in June of 2009 and will be completed during the first quarter of 2010. When the study is completed, results will be posted at www.vaporizeyouranxiety.com.

Dr. Telch told me that currently the gold standard of

anxiety treatment within the field of psychology is cognitive therapy. It is going to be very interesting to see what kind of effect size, meaning the amount of measurable change, that people can achieve using the *Pure Awareness* Techniques. If the participants in the study have results like we have been seeing with other people with anxiety over the years we may be able to set a new standard for research and treatment of anxiety, even though we don't consider **Human Software Engineering** to be treatment, but rather just training. While many people who have had years of cognitive therapy have said after going through a couple of sessions of HSE that it was vastly more helpful to them than 10 years of traditional therapy, it will be fascinating to see if this subjective difference is scientifically measureable.

To get updates by email you can join our email list at http://vaporizeyouranxiety.com/research.html

CHAPTER 27

Beyond Anxiety: How the *Pure Awareness* Techniques Can Change Your Life

First and foremost, using both the SEE Technique and the CORE Technique will liberate you from being the victim of anxiety. But the techniques to **Vaporize Your Anxiety** are about much more than stopping anxiety. They're about becoming someone who is more and more grounded in the experience of *Pure Awareness*, the essential nature of what you are. They're about becoming someone who is emotionally competent and emotionally mature. Believe it or not, vaporizing your anxiety is actually one of the smallest rewards that you will be getting from learning and using the exercises in this book and becoming competent at using these techniques.

As you use the CORE technique more and more, you'll

find that you're in the process of dismantling many of the strategies you use to avoid of being overwhelmed. This will allow you to start being more true to yourself, to start trusting and consistently acting on your intuition, and to become much less judgmental of others and yourself. Those around you will instantly recognize this and notice that you have an energy and vitality in your life that wasn't there before.

In Malcolm Gladwell's wonderful book *Blink*, he describes the amazing things that happen when people act on their intuition. Multi-million dollar pieces already purchased by major museums have been exposed as frauds. Lives of heart-attack victims have been saved by ER doctors who trusted their own intuition more than the machinery designed to diagnose their patients. Time and time again, major cultural shifts have been the result of people's split-second decisions that were based on two things: strong intuition and immediate action with *no second-guessing*. As a result of regularly using the SEE and CORE Techniques, you will be more attuned to your intuition.

Another thing that will happen to you as you practice the *Pure Awareness* Techniques regularly is that you will gain the capacity to be fully present for everything that comes your way in life. One of the primary difficulties in intimate relationships is that one or both people have a hard time actually *being there* with the other person.

They are distracted by their own concerns and fears. As a result, their partners can end up feeling lonely and left out. Working through your incomplete emotional experiences will allow you to really show up for your life and the people in it, and you'll be appreciated for it in ways you may never have imagined.

> When you can feel fully, you'll find that you can stack the cards in your favor by working on resolving your backlog of emotional pain and fear before stressful events even have a chance to trigger these emotions.

What all of these things have in common is that they require the ability to feel fully. When you develop that skill, you'll find that you can stack the cards in your favor

> The good news is that your database of fear and emotional pain is finite. It does not go on forever. That means that every time you complete one of these unresolved experiences, it is truly vaporized—that one isn't coming back. You are becoming more and more free of the underlying causes of anxiety. Soon it will be a thing of the past.

by working on resolving your backlog of emotional pain and fear before stressful events even have a chance to trigger them. These are archived fears that left unvaporized can cause you to feel anxious in the future.

And remember, your ability and effectiveness in using the CORE Technique will get better and better with practice. Your body will be getting increasingly free of fear and emotional pain. This builds a positively reinforcing cycle in which each time you resolve a fearful or painful emotion you gain even more access to your true self, which in turn encourages you to work on resolving more and more of that backlog of emotional pain. You will experience a continuous and cumulative upgrading of your capacity to feel and be present. As you resolve each held fear, emotional pain, stress or trauma, it opens your awareness more and more to *Pure Awareness*, that state of blissful purity where you can finally be what and who you truly are.

CHAPTER 28

The GAP Technique: Easily Accessing Inner Peace

As someone who suffers from anxiety, it may be encouraging for you to hear that I have developed a technique that will allow you to easily access inner peace. I call it the GAP technique. GAP stands for *Greater Awareness Place*, and the GAP Technique is a way to quickly and directly experience a state of inner peace in a matter of moments. It's a very simple technique that anyone can do. In this section of the book we'll go into the description of the GAP Technique in a detail and also explain when to use it, how to handle thoughts that come up during it, and cover some special applications.

Recent scientific research in neuroscience confirms that there are periods of inactivity in the brain that correspond to the gaps between thoughts. And if you pay attention to your thoughts for a while, just observing them as they come and go, you'll notice that they are not continuous. One thought begins, has a particular duration, and then ends before the next thought begins. It is the gap between the thoughts that we are interested in noticing here, because it is in those gaps that *Pure Awareness* resides.

Practicing the GAP Technique can rapidly bring you the clear, direct experience of *Pure Awareness*, which in turn brings a profound sense of inner peace, centeredness, relaxation, and expansion of awareness. As you gradually increase your familiarity with *Pure Awareness*, you begin to sense a shift in your sense of who you are. You move from thinking of yourself as an anxious, isolated individual to experiencing yourself as the totality of *Pure Awareness*, connected to all others on Earth and alive to the connectedness that is our true state of being.

This would be a good time to take a few minutes to experience *Pure Awareness* again. One of the simplest and most effective ways to do this is to listen to an audio recording of me guiding someone through it. You can just follow along and do the technique yourself by simply listening and following the simple instructions. I've made a recording available for you in the resources section of the *Vaporize Your Anxiety* web site. Just visit www.vaporizeyouranxiety.com/resources.html.

If you don't have Internet access, you can have someone

read you the script below. Because the GAP Technique takes the mind inward to a place of deep quietness, this will work better than going back and forth between reading and listening. Opening your eyes in the middle of this process, especially several times, will tend to disrupt the process of going inward. So do keep them closed.

Exercise: GAP – Greater Awareness Place – Experiencing the silent background in which thoughts occur.

The purpose of this exercise is to shift the attention from an outward direction to an inward direction so that it is possible to experience the essential nature of awareness itself. An analogy is useful here. Think of thoughts occurring in the mind as similar to clouds blowing by on a partly cloudy day. The clouds are like thoughts and they occur in the background of the blue sky.

In an analogous way, thoughts occur in the mind in a silent background. There has to be a silent background because if it were filled with other experiences you wouldn't be able to hear the thoughts!

It is easy enough to see the sky. Simply look off to the side of the clouds and there it is. Similarly, it is easy to experience the silent background in which thoughts occur by simply looking off to the side of the thoughts and noticing the background of silence. This silent background is your own awareness. This is your awareness being aware of itself.

Have someone read you the following script:

(Instructions for the person reading: *If you were the reader for the SEE and/or CORE Technique earlier in the book, this will be familiar to you. The approach is the same: read the* "bold sections in quotation marks" out loud *and read the italicized sections silently to yourself.)*

Start here:

"**Please sit comfortably and close your eyes.**"

Wait for about half a minute.

"**Notice that with your eyes closed you experience several kinds of things. You hear my voice, you may notice feeling your body sitting in the chair, you may notice other noises or sensations, and you will notice that there are thoughts coming to you.**"

Pause

"**Notice that the thoughts are occurring in a background of silence.**"

Pause

"**You can notice the background of silence by simply looking off to the side of the thoughts and there it is.**"

Now wait for about half a minute.

"**Notice that this silent background is truly empty. There is nothing there. It's just *Pure Awareness* without the awareness of anything else.**

Pause

"**As you notice the silent background in which the thoughts are occurring, you will notice that** you can be aware of it even while the thoughts are coming and going. Allow yourself to simply favor noticing that silent background. Immerse yourself in that silence."

Wait about one minute

"If you find that you have become absorbed in thinking, at the moment when you notice this, simply bring your attention back to the silent background by again looking off to the side of the thoughts."

Wait one to two minutes here.

"Okay. When you're ready, open your eyes."

When the person has opened their eyes please ask them the following:

What did you experience?

What was it like?

What are the attributes of that background of silence?

You may get responses such as: "It's quiet." "It's peaceful." "It's expansive." "It's pleasant." "It's relaxing." "It's very nice."

This is the end of the script for guiding someone through the GAP Technique.

From here, you can begin reading the book again yourself.

Take a moment to jot down the answers to the three questions from above. If you'd like to add anything, feel free. Don't try to force it or make it more than it was. Just let your answers flow naturally.

What did you experience?

_____

_____

_____

_____

_____

_____

What are the attributes of that background of silence?

_____

_____

_____

_____

_____

_____

What was it like, compared to your experiences of anxiety?

_____

_____

_____

_____

_____

_____

Now that you have experienced your own *Pure Awareness*, it is easy to notice that *Pure Awareness* is always there, lively in the background, even with your eyes open and with the activity of experiencing the objects of the senses. Can you still feel the presence of *Pure Awareness*? Is there anything lacking in the experience of that *Pure Awareness*? Is there any sense of anxiety or fear while you are in *Pure Awareness*? Is there anything that you could not do from this place? If you're like most people, tasting *Pure Awareness* is like simultaneously becoming aware of true peace and true power.

If you aren't sure whether you had a clear experience of *Pure Awareness* or not, don't worry. This is common. After all, remember that every experience you have is an experience of some THING, some object of perception. Our lives are so focused in an outward direction that we tend not to realize or remember that this silent *Pure Awareness* is the essence of what we are. Because there is literally *no-thing* there, *Pure Awareness* can seem very abstract and so completely unlike our other experiences, that when you first experience it you may not be sure that you did.

> Our lives are so focused in an outward direction that we tend not to realize or remember that this silent Pure Awareness is the essence of what we are.

After all, our only database of experiences prior to a few moments ago was of the experience of things as things. So if you aren't sure if you experienced it, just try going through the exercise again. Remember, you're not trying to experience something that's an object. It's just the silent witness of your experiences, just your awareness itself, that with which you experience everything else. It is the thing upon which all your experiences occur.

Now that you have directly experienced *Pure Awareness* you may see what I mean by how simple and easy it is to have this experience. This is because there is nowhere to go, there is nothing to do. It is just a matter of noticing the background of silence in which your thoughts and perceptions are occurring. That's it. It is simply your own awareness being aware of itself!

Now that you have experienced *Pure Awareness* by accessing it using the GAP Technique, I'd like to give you a little bit more insight about the technique, and how to get the most out of it.

MORE ON THE GAP TECHNIQUE

Although you now know the basics of how to do the GAP Technique, there are some subtleties that will be helpful to know about. It is good to start by allowing yourself to become aware of thoughts occurring in your mind. You simply notice that your thoughts are occurring in a background of silence. Normally we don't pay any attention to the background of silence in which the thoughts are occurring. When we're listening to music in our living room, we don't pay attention to the fact (or even realize) that this music is actually playing against a background of silence, and that the silent background is what makes hearing the music possible in the first place. Likewise, when we go to the movies we become absorbed in the images that are present on the screen, but we don't pay attention to or even remember the blank white screen that allows the images to be seen. Even though the white screen is there, we don't see it when it is covered up by the images and activity of the movie.

Similarly, the background of silence in which our thoughts occur is usually *covered up* by the *volume* of the sounds or images of our thoughts. Our thoughts are active, have meaning, sometimes have emotions associated with them, and they are certainly more engaging at the level of *content* than the background of silence in which they are occurring. So thoughts tend to attract our attention more than the silence does. Like the white screen at the movie theater, we usually don't even know it is there until we actually put our attention there to experience it—as you just have.

It is an amazing thing: if we want to experience our essential nature—our very own *Pure Awareness*—it's a simple matter of *looking off to the side of the thoughts* and noticing that these thoughts are occurring in a background of silence. Interestingly enough, this can be done even when the mind is racing with lots of thoughts.

THOUGHTS, THOUGHTS AND MORE THOUGHTS— WHAT CAN I DO?

> Having lots of thoughts is *not* a barrier to experiencing Pure Awareness

A common feature of people who are anxious is that they feel bombarded by thoughts. While practicing the GAP Technique, you may become concerned that you're getting absorbed in thinking, and that this seems to be getting in the way of the experience of *Pure Awareness*. It's important to understand the role of thoughts during the GAP Technique and to know how to handle them.

The answer is that there is nothing to handle. I'm not making a bad joke—having thoughts occur is really *not* a barrier to experiencing *Pure Awareness*. It is perfectly possible to experience *Pure Awareness* and have thoughts occurring at the same time. It's just a matter of noticing what you favor with your attention. It's certainly true that we are deeply habituated to noticing our thoughts. I would go so far as to say that just about everyone seems to be addicted to thinking. In fact, my experience is that many people actually use being absorbed in thinking as a "drug of choice" to avoid feeling things.

> Many people use being absorbed in thinking as a drug of choice to avoid feeling things.

But this doesn't mean you can't experience the background of silence even while thoughts are occurring. You can simply choose to shift your attention from noticing thoughts to noticing the background of silence. You can allow yourself to really immerse your attention in that silent background. When you do this, it is quite easy to simply allow yourself to shift your attention away from the thoughts and more toward noticing the background of silence. Just as you can read a book with birds chirping outside or with the hum of traffic on the freeway a few blocks way, you have the ability to direct your awareness to favor noticing one thing more than something else. It's just that we are so deeply conditioned to only notice our thoughts that most of us don't even realize there is a silent background in which the thoughts are occurring.

As you practice noticing *Pure Awareness*—that background of silence in which the thoughts occur—you may begin to have some extended periods of very clear experiences of *Pure Awareness*. Sometimes there won't seem to be any thoughts at all. The thoughts may seem to fade so deeply into the background that you hardly notice them. When this happens it can be a very powerful and satisfying experience. You will feel deeply refreshed and fully alive while also feeling deeply rested and relaxed.

As you practice the GAP Technique for longer periods of time, say 10 to 20 minutes, you may also have experiences of becoming absorbed in thinking for what seem to be long periods of many minutes. Sometimes when this happens people think that they are doing the GAP Technique incorrectly or that something is wrong with what they are doing. Nothing could be further from the truth.

> When you become lost to thoughts during the GAP Technique this is actually because the technique is working beautifully!

This may seem like a strange proposition. How could it be working if the idea is to experience the GAP and not the thoughts? There is a very special answer to this question that will allow you to take a whole new attitude towards the thoughts that occur while you are doing the GAP Technique. Here it is:

When you shift your attention to noticing the background of silence in which the thoughts are occurring, you are favoring noticing a state within you that's much less active than the active mind—the one that's usually busy thinking thoughts. As you shift your attention to noticing *Pure Awareness* you will sometimes notice that you feel very relaxed. This is because you are naturally giving less energy to the mental activity of thinking.

We tend to think of our body and mind as separate things, but the truth is that they are both parts of one wholeness—*who we are*. When we begin to notice the silent background of *Pure Awareness* and naturally experience less mental activity, an amazing thing happens: our mind settles down. And as our mind settles down, our body naturally settles down as well. This allows us to feel deeply relaxed. During this relaxation it is also natural for the body to begin to release any stresses or strains that may have accumulated.

When stresses and strains begin to be released in the body, this creates movement or activity in the body. This activity naturally creates new movement and activity in our mind because, as we've already noted, the mind and body are intimately connected. This means becoming absorbed in thoughts while practicing the GAP Technique is actually a very positive by-product of the phenomenon of releasing stresses and strains.

I've also had people fall asleep during the GAP Technique. This might seem like a very different kind of response from becoming absorbed in thoughts, but it is actually the same thing in a different wrapper. It's just the body releasing accumulated fatigue, so you fall asleep. It's all quite natural. When you do the GAP Technique, your body will take the opportunity to give itself what it needs, whether that means releasing stress, fatigue or other energies. This is a wonderful example of the naturally integrated functioning of mind and body.

So if you have lots of thoughts during a particular session of the GAP Technique, it actually means that you have successfully accessed the GAP and settled the mind down, even if it's only for a short time. It means that the body is releasing some stresses and strains. This in turn is creating the activity of thinking in a strong enough way that your mind becomes quite occupied with this activity. This is experienced as thoughts in the mind. It's not from doing it wrong. On the contrary, it is from doing the technique correctly!

So don't have the attitude that thoughts shouldn't be there. It's natural for them to be there. It is also natural for you to shift from noticing *Pure Awareness* to noticing the thoughts. When this happens, here's what you can do about it:

When you notice that you have been absorbed in thinking, don't bother to chastise yourself. Actually, something good has just happened—you've released some stress. When the body has released enough stress that you become aware that you've been thinking, now it is time to go back into the GAP and experience *Pure Awareness* again. When you become aware that you were thinking, gently shift your attention back to noticing the background of silence in which the thoughts are occurring.

Simply allow for the naturalness of both thinking and noticing *Pure Awareness* in the background of silence. There is a natural shifting back and forth between noticing *Pure Awareness* and being absorbed in thinking. The idea, after all, is to cultivate a clean inner landscape using the CORE Technique and to become completely familiar with *Pure Awareness* using the GAP Technique. Eventually, you will no longer lose the experience of *Pure Awareness*, and it won't be overshadowed by thoughts or by anything else.

When you develop this state of being, you come to experience the presence of *Pure Awareness* all the time, 24/7/365—it never goes away. And that's what we're after. When you reach this state, which can develop quite quickly by regularly using the *Pure Awareness* Techniques, you will be able to maintain the experience of *Pure Awareness* not only while you're having thoughts, but even while you're having intense experiences of pleasure or pain. In this state you're never lost to your experiences, and you experience a shift from being an individual to being *Pure Awareness*, which is the true reality of what you really are. In this state anxiety doesn't exist. It permanently becomes a non-issue and you are never anxious again.

WHEN TO USE THE GAP TECHNIQUE

Just like we sometimes don't consciously realize when our bodies are thirsty, when they would benefit from water, we sometimes don't realize when we would benefit from an encounter with *Pure Awareness*. And just like water is necessary to the optimal functioning of our bodies, *Pure Awareness* is necessary to the optimal functioning of our selves.

You can use the GAP Technique whenever you like, whenever you want to experience *Pure Awareness*. Some people like to make a regular practice of the GAP Technique and use it as a form of meditation that they do once or twice a day, typically in the morning and evening. Another time you may find the GAP Technique particularly beneficial is before doing something where you would benefit from being in a place of wholeness, such as giving a presentation or having an important meeting. Or you might just like to take a moment out of your busy, stressful day to experience *Pure Awareness*. It's a rejuvenating experience! As you practice it, you will cultivate the presence of *Pure Awareness* in your life. You can find the frequency and duration that suits your individual tastes and desires for developing *Pure Awareness*.

Although making the GAP Technique a regular practice is highly recommended, don't overdo it. Sitting around doing the GAP Technique for hours at a time may not be the best plan for integrating the state of *Pure Awareness* into your life. What is optimal is to toggle back and forth between becoming familiar with *Pure Awareness* by doing the GAP Technique for short periods of time and then engaging in your daily activities. Balance is the key, and introducing the GAP Technique into your daily routine starts you on a path of integrating *Pure Awareness* into your life experience. The value of doing this is enormous.

The GAP Technique is also very useful during *Core Dynamics* Coaching sessions whenever someone has become overly identified with things in their life. People tend to become identified and attached to their possessions, the people and relationships in their life, their thoughts and ideas, their emotions, expectations, reactions, stories and self-definitions. It is in the nature of human conditioning to become identified with both our inner and outer experiences and lose the sense of connection to our own essential nature—*Pure Awareness*.

You can use the GAP technique to gently guide yourself back to the experience of *Pure Awareness* when you need to experience the inner reference of who you really are. It is a great experiential antidote when you have slipped into getting the sense of who you are from anything other than *Pure Awareness*. This quickly re-establishes the inner sense of being grounded in one's Self. Many forms of attachment, struggle, and suffering just melt away and are recognized for the illusions that they are and problems that they have caused. The GAP Technique is a simple and quick way to bring yourself out of all of the *Core Dynamics* in the categories that we call *Looking for Yourself Where You Are Not* and *Trying to Force an Outcome*. If there is a charged emotion associated with the attachment, then you can access *Pure Awareness* using the SEE Technique.

Sanyama and the GPS Technique

My dear friend and colleague Michael Stratford, who is the Director of the *Core Dynamics* Coach Training Program for Great Life Technologies and who co-teaches this program with me, came up with a wonderful use of the GAP Technique that he calls "GPS." He had learned the GAP Technique and was practicing it regularly in order to cultivate a greater experiential familiarity with *Pure Awareness*.

On New Year's Day, 2007 he was thinking about what was coming in the year ahead, and experiencing some uncertainty. While doing the GAP technique that morning, he had the idea to go into *Pure Awareness* and just ask a question. What, if anything, should he do to support bringing about the things he envisioned happening in the year ahead? He just relaxed into *Pure Awareness* and listened, and some surprising answers came to him that he never would have thought of otherwise. Those answers gave him an entirely new direction for his business and coaching career. He suddenly got a level of clarity that allowed him to end his involvement with a coaching school he'd been working with for a long time, and instead focus his time and energy in new directions.

He was quite amazed by the experience, and immediately began using it with his clients. Once Michael has guided someone into *Pure Awareness* using the GAP Technique, he suggests that they simply ask any important question they'd like to have some guidance about, and encourages them to wait and see what happens. Using this technique with his clients, he found that they would typically get some kind of "knowing" or even very clear thoughts or ideas coming to them that they had never even considered before. On one hand, they might discover that there is nothing at all to do; on the other hand, they might receive guidance about taking specific actions to bring about a particular outcome.

When Michael first told me about this technique, he said, "*Dropping a question into Pure Awareness is like putting a destination into a GPS (Global Positioning System) in a car. All of a sudden the path to where you want to go becomes perfectly clear.*" Based on this analogy, we decided to call this technique GPS, for **Gentle Provocation System**.

This variation on the GAP Technique was a true revelation for me because the process is very similar to an ancient technique described by Yogi Patanjali, an Indian sage who is thought by some to be the father of the entire field of Yoga. Patanjali described a technique called *Sanyama*, a Sanskrit word meaning *consciousness that knows only truth*. Sanyama refers to a kind of meditative awareness in which you first experience *Pure Awareness* and then have a quiet intention while in this state and let it go into *Pure Awareness*. The outcome of this practice is the development of *Sidhis*, which translates as *perfections*.

The idea is that when you have a thought at the level of Sanyama, it activates the support of the laws of nature—the full power of the infinite potential that is latent in *Pure Awareness*. Practicing Sanyama is a powerful way to bring yourself into alignment with these laws of nature. In Sanyama, one does not command the laws of nature, but learns how to become one with them. Incredibly enough, Michael seems to have independently rediscovered some of Patanjali's insights.

Another interesting use of GPS is to access any remaining energy of an incompletion. What you do is simply ask to become aware of any remaining energy of any incompletion that you might be holding onto. In this case, you're asking not for ideas or insights, but simply to be made more aware of any incomplete energy that you might still be inadvertently holding in your body.

A recent example of this comes from my experience with a client who had a very subtle fear of being vulnerable that, without being aware of it, was in fact holding him back from being even more fully successful in his life. He was teaching a course and he was finding that the students weren't responding and participating as much as he would like during each session. He was already quite familiar with the *Core Dynamics*, so rather than blaming the students, he took this as a cue that perhaps there was some subtle way he might be contributing to or even creating the problem with participation.

As he was sharing this experience with me we were able to identify that he had a subtle inner fear of being vulnerable or exposed and we realized that his students were mirroring this fear to him. I suggested that he go into the GAP and then make a request to be shown any remaining energy of the fear of being vulnerable. I instructed him to notice the energy that came up in his body and then to shift to the CORE Technique when he became aware of where it was being held. I explained to him that as the energy dissolved he would either notice that it was gone or that he might become absorbed in thinking thoughts about something else. He did this, and after a time reported that he had indeed become absorbed in thinking. When he became aware of this, he then went back into *Pure Awareness* using the GAP technique and again made the request to be shown any remaining energy related to the fear of vulnerability. After several iterations of this process, he again asked to be shown any remaining energy of the fear of being vulnerable, and this time nothing presented itself. It was just quiet and peaceful inside.

He then had the realization that he could now be fully present and self-expressed under any circumstances and felt completely free of any fear of vulnerability. The release of this deeply held but hidden fear was profound for him. When it was gone, he just laughed and laughed for several minutes because it was such a huge relief to be free of something that he hadn't even known he had been holding onto his whole life!

The key is to do this technique repeatedly until the point that when you ask to be shown any remaining energy of the emotion you get... nothing. Just to be sure you make the request again. If you get nothing again, you are really complete with it!

GPS is a great way to make sure you have really felt every aspect of any previously incomplete emotional experience. It is also a great way to get access to incompletions that you can't name or describe with words. It is a subtle and powerful addition to the *Pure Awareness* Techniques.

CHAPTER 30

Getting Past the Gatekeeper

> Gatekeepers come from the fear of
> losing a part of the sense of who you are.

Sometimes the energy of the feeling that you are holding inside doesn't seem to get completed no matter how much you use the CORE Technique and feel into the heart of it.

Why does this sometimes happen and what can we do about it?

Some emotions have been with us so long that they feel like they are a part of who we are—like our nose or hands. They aren't of course, but these feelings can be so compelling that when we go to feel into them to complete them, there is another part of us that is afraid that we will lose something that feels like it a part of us and we won't know who we are any more. There is a fear of the uncertainty that will come if that feeling we've been holding onto all these years really does go away.

If we could articulate it we might say to ourselves:

"If I complete the experience of this emotion, then part of me won't be there any more. I'll lose a part of myself and that's really scary. I don't like having this emotion but then again at least it's familiar. If it's gone I won't know who I am anymore."

When the energy won't resolve using the CORE Technique, no matter how much we try, we call the thing that is keeping us from resolving it a *Gatekeeper*. It's like having someone standing in front of the door who won't let you in. You just  can't get in. Gatekeepers are usually the energy of the fear of letting go—in this case, letting go of something that has felt like a part of you for so long that you won't know who you are if it's gone. In the *Core Dynamics* model, our set of insights into the nature of preverbal conditioning, we call this the Core Dynamic of Resisting Change.

When we run into a Gatekeeper, the CORE Technique won't feel like it is working. When this happens there is a way to get to *Pure Awareness* through a side door. This is the SEE Technique. And in these circumstances it can work really well. As you know, SEE stands for Side Entrance Expansion. Rather than going into the CORE of the energy of the feeling, this approach does the opposite. It takes your attention out to the outer edges of the feeling. But then instead of being stuck in the outer edges of the feeling we take our awareness even a little bit further. When you do this you can access the silent background in which the experience of the emotion is occurring. It is a variation on the GAP technique.

All experiences are occurring in the background of silence that is *Pure Awareness*. And that background of silence is so vast, so unlimited that anything you experience will be smaller than it. If you take your awareness out past the outer edges of the field of the energy of the feeling, then you can access the background of silence in which even intense emotions such as this are being experienced.

The background of silence that is our own *Pure Awareness* is a field of lively pure potential that in itself isn't a *thing*. It is that with which we experience everything. It is our very aliveness. And because it is limitless and easily accessible you can always get to it out beyond the outer edges of *any* experience.

I was recently giving a demonstration of this technique to someone making an inquiry about some of the products and programs offered by Great Life Technologies. She said that she was stuck in an ongoing state of anxiety. She had been read my book, *Pure Awareness—Five Simple Techniques for Experiencing Your Essential Nature* and she had already been using the CORE Technique regularly. But the underlying fear simply wasn't going away. As we began to talk about her experience, she very quickly got in touch with the fear that was creating her anxious feelings. I asked her if she would like to have a breakthrough with this issue right now. She said that she would. She said that the energy of the fear was so huge that it was all consuming. She was lost to it. The fear had her in its grip.

Taking her through the SEE Technique, I asked her to take her awareness out to the outer edges of the fear. Then I asked her to go even a little bit further and notice that out beyond the outer edges of the field of energy of the fear there was quietness. This quietness is the silent background in which the experience of the fear was occurring. As she started to experience it I told her to simply favor noticing the silent background instead of continuing to be absorbed in the fear. I said, "Notice how vast that background of silence is. Notice that this vastness of the silent background is much bigger than the field of energy of the fear." She acknowledged that it was and that she could feel that. I then invited her to immerse herself in the silent background and as she did, she reported that the energy of the fear started to subside. It was vaporizing. Within a few minutes the fear was completely gone. When we checked in to see if there was any anxiety left she said, "What anxiety!?"

When we access *Pure Awareness* using the SEE Technique, whatever was causing us to be so absorbed in the emotion, so completely in its grip, softens and begins to let go.

This is because when we are stuck inside the experience of the emotion, our awareness has collapsed into the sense that we *are* the emotion. We have become so identified with the emotion that it feels like we have become that emotion. It's all consuming. In those moments when we are caught in the grip of the emotion, it seems that any other sense of ourselves that we might once have had gets completely overshadowed by the intensity of the experience of the emotion. And if we have had this going on for a long time, it is no wonder that it feels like the emotion is a part of our self-definition. No wonder we have a hard time letting it go.

But when we use the SEE Technique, as we begin to experience *Pure Awareness* in the background of silence in which the intense emotion is occurring, we start to regain the experience of our essential nature. This gives us the comforting feeling of having come home to a totally safe place that is peaceful and nurturing.

The sense of complete identification with that feeling begins to vaporize.

The SEE Technique is a wonderful way to overcome the resistance to change and the fear of the loss of sense of self. It is a marvelous remedy for vaporizing Gatekeepers.

But it is also possible to have gatekeepers when using the SEE Technique. When this happens, instead of the energy fading away completely, there's a feeling that it is still there. Another way that it happens during the SEE Technique is that while you are attempting to notice the outer edge of the energy field and find the quietness that is out beyond the edge of it, the energy field feels like it is pulling you back into itself. This is similar to when during the CORE Technique the energy doesn't seem to be able to be completed. In both cases there is clearly something keeping the energy of the emotion in tact. What is it that is holding this energy in place? Again, it is the fear that if I really let this go then I will lose something that's been around for a long time and that feels like a part of me. I'm afraid to let it go. These are the gatekeepers and the remedy is to first identify the fear of not knowing who you will be any more if you let it go and then use the SEE Technique on that fear.

The result of using the SEE Technique on the fear of not knowing who you will be if you let it go is that when you get your awareness all the way out to the outer edge of the energy field you will again be in *Pure Awareness*.

Because *Pure Awareness* is the ***real*** essence of what you truly are, it is the long lost ***you*** that you've been wanting as a stable inner reference. The moment that you step across the outer edge of the energy field of this fear, in that moment you have an amazing experience. You are suddenly in the contrasting experience of actually being your true Self.

Because you are now directly experiencing the reality of what you are, immediately juxtaposed to the illusion of something that you thought was a real part of you but isn't, the illusory notion that you were holding onto just can't maintain its appearance of being real anymore. After all, you are now experiencing what you really are. Needing to hold onto something that isn't really you in the face of this doesn't seem so compelling. Typically the energy of the fear of losing the sense of who you are gets vaporized in that moment and simply melts away into nothingness.

Dealing with gatekeepers is not something for a beginner with the *Pure Awareness* Techniques. In fact if you are struggling with doing these techniques or you have some energy that when using either the SEE or the CORE Technique just won't go away, you may want to work with someone trained to guide people through these techniques who is skilled at removing gatekeepers. You can learn about that in the Additional Resources section at the end of the book.

CHAPTER 31

So, You Don't Think You Have Anxiety?

Anxiety in its varying degrees of severity is probably much more common than the statistics indicate. This is because many people are so used to getting anxious under different circumstances that we just think it's normal. And we become resigned to it because we haven't had the tools to break free from all those anxious patterns. You may get anxious at times and even though you don't like it, you have accepted it because you don't want to take medication for it and therapy didn't work for you either. So you just live with it. But now, that's not necessary.

Because anxiety can show up in so many areas of life I'm going to be dedicating a separate book to each of the most common areas in which people tend to have anxiety. We'll be examining the specific ways in which people get anxious in different life circumstances and showing you how to use the *Pure Awareness* Techniques to resolve each of these variations of being anxious. The reason I am doing this is for just the point I've made above. You may be so accustomed to having anxiety about something that you won't recognize that you could be vaporizing it and enjoying a greatly enhanced life as a result.

Maybe you already know what makes you anxious, but so often even that isn't completely clear. So this series of books is designed to help you get in touch with and then deal with the specific areas of your life in which you may have become resigned to having anxiety.

> Your story of my helping you to resolve your personal anxiety issue could be in my next book!

VAPORIZE YOUR ANXIETY BOOK SERIES

What we are going to do as we begin to write each of these additional books in the *Vaporize Your Anxiety* series have some live teleconferences or webinars in which I will work with people on anxiety issues that they have that fall under the topic of that book. We'll use the appropriate *Pure Awareness* Technique right then and there on the conference call to *Vaporize Your Anxiety*. For example if we are working on the Holiday Anxiety book we'll have some calls to address how to overcome your anxieties about family gatherings, financial pressures, looking good, doing it all perfectly, time limitations, etc.

As you read through the initial list of titles and topics that we have planned for the series, find ones that you can relate to. Let me know what your anxiety issue is and which book topic you feel is related by e-mailing me at includeme@vaporizeyouranxiety.com. When it is time to start on that book, we'll invite you to a free teleconference with others who want to be included, and I'll work with as many participants as I can to help them resolve their anxiety right during the session. You'll need to sign a release that lets me use your case as an example in the book, but that will be fun for you and maybe yours will be included. Everyone who is included will of course get acknowledged in the book. Here's one of the titles and some of the topics that will be covered in this upcoming book:

Vaporize Your Holiday Anxiety

- Do you experience anxiety as the holidays are approaching?

- Any worries about how to manage the extended family not to mention blended families? Will everyone get along?

- How about financial challenges, particularly in the current economic conditions? Are you conflicted between wanting to get special presents and needing to keep the spending in line with reduced income? Will we be able to get enough for the kids? We don't want to disappoint them.

- And how about all of the costs of entertaining, and traveling to see the relatives?

- Who shall we go see this year and on which days? How can we afford it this year? Should we put it on a credit card? But then what will we do when the bills come in?

- And how are we going to find time for all of the socializing, especially with the new demands at work since the cutbacks? And what if I get laid off or let go. The company's really hurting right now and I don't know if I've really got a job or not.

- How about the need to look good and have everything be perfect? What about the house? Is it in need of some sprucing up? Can we really afford to do that? But it looks so awful if we don't.

- What about holiday decorations? Will they be good enough?

- What am I possibly going to get for Mom this year?

Can you relate to any of these? They're pretty common, and there are so many more. Drop me an email at includeme@vaporizeyouranxiety.com if you'd like to *Vaporize Your Holiday Anxiety*, or if there are additional areas that you'd like to see us include.

- Vaporize Your Financial Anxiety
- Vaporize Your Sales Anxiety
- Vaporize Your PTSD Anxiety
- Vaporize Your Small Business Anxiety
- Vaporize Your Menopause Anxiety
- Vaporize Your Mid-Life Crisis Anxiety
- Vaporize Your Performance Anxiety
- Vaporize Your Academic Anxiety
- Vaporize Your Parenting Anxiety
- Vaporize Your Pregnancy Anxiety
- Vaporize Your Workplace Anxiety
- Vaporize Your Family Anxiety

Conclusion

Over the years, it has become clear to me that the problems people have in their lives are almost always caused by the loss of the experience of Wholeness—the loss of the connection to their essential nature, or *Pure Awareness*. The real answer to moving beyond your problems is to regain that experience, which is your birthright. And that's just what the techniques in this book are about. They are about rediscovering and reclaiming the unique human experience of Wholeness.

Now that you have learned, experienced and practiced the *Pure Awareness* Techniques to *Vaporize Your Anxiety* you may already have made major progress toward resolving your anxiety. As I've said throughout the book, to successfully *Vaporize Your Anxiety* you must actually do the techniques. The thing to keep in mind is that most people need to practice them for some time in order to thoroughly clean house and cleanse their inner emotional landscape of all of the emotional baggage they've accumulated throughout their lives. So don't stop before you've practiced enough, because what you'll find is that when you've truly completed the experience of all of those incomplete emotional energies and extracted yourself from your absorption in projections of possible negative outcomes onto the future, you simply won't feel anxious anymore.

My wish for you is that by learning and using the techniques in this book you will grant yourself a life completely free from anxiety; a life of freedom, peace, and true enjoyment of all the richness that your life has to offer. You have the natural ability to do this within you. That's what's possible when you really integrate these techniques into your life.

From the foreword by Jack Canfield to *The Power of How* by Tom Stone

I was giving a seminar for a local business in Fairfield, IA in December 1993. The company was using the large meeting room at the Fairfield Best Western Motel for the seminar. Tom Stone happened to be having lunch that day at the motel's restaurant called the Wild Rose. I was having lunch there as well with some of the participants from the seminar. A friend of Tom's was among them and as she and I were walking back from the salad bar, she stopped and introduced me to Tom.

"They tell me you are a walking miracle," I said. Less than five weeks before this Tom had been shot in the chest with a .44 caliber hand gun by a stranger and had survived it. Now he was up and walking around, even having lunch at the restaurant. Tom's friend had already mentioned his incident to me. She had also told me a little bit about Tom's expert use of kinesiology also known as muscle testing. The three of us chatted and arranged for Tom to come to the motel that evening and give me a private session. I also invited Tom to join the group for the afternoon portion of my self-esteem seminar.

Tom did drop in for a while in the afternoon and learned that I was already very familiar with kinesiology. I had been intrigued with it for quite some time and often demonstrated its use in my classes.

That evening when Tom arrived, I only had an hour before I was going to be picked up and taken to another appointment so we quickly got started. My familiarity with muscle checking made me immediately comfortable with the process. As the session progressed, Tom quickly identified what was going on in me.

"What's bothering you?" he asked.

I want to affect the lives of a larger number of people. I want to help more people and have a bigger impact. I feel like I'm on a plateau, that I am settling for less than I really want. We then spent some time discussing what it was that I wanted and crafting a positive intention statement. It read as follows:

"I have a major impact in the world, bringing love and empowerment to large numbers of people and I receive the natural benefits of this. I have the courage to take the necessary stands to manifest my vision."

We muscle tested me for this intention and I was "switched off." Tom explained that this indicated that there were "inner conflicts" that were blocking me from manifesting this intention as my reality.

Tom then proceeded to identify these inner conflicts. They ranged from areas of stress in my life having to do with money, to an earlier unpleasant experience, to unconscious ways that I was compensating for not getting the love I wanted, to limiting beliefs. I was amazed at the depth and scope of the issues that were blocking me. I was also fascinated with the incredible accuracy and speed with which Tom identified these patterns. I knew that muscle checking was a great tool, but I had never before seen it used in such a refined and precise manner.

The whole process took just about an hour. I was quite impressed. And I felt somehow different, like something inside had shifted. But would this really make a difference in my being able to broaden my influence and serve millions of people?

My first book, *Chicken Soup for the Soul,* was already written and published when I had that session with Tom. But it was only in the months that followed that the sales really started to take off and the book became the first in a series of best sellers. There are of course many other things that influenced this, but the simple procedures that Tom helped me with during that hour seemed to make a real difference between staying stuck in some old patterns and being able to break free and create what I really wanted for myself. One thing I vividly remember is that Tom "debugged" me for being a "packrat!" When I got home I cleaned out everything in my house and threw away literally about 15 garbage bags of accumulated, unneeded stuff!

Since that time, Tom has truly become a master at using kinesiology to help people identify what is blocking them. He has worked with thousands of people helping them to clarify their life purpose, awaken their unique talents, and helping them remove their inner barriers to having the success in their lives that they truly want. Also in the intervening years he has been pioneering a whole new field that he calls **Human Software Engineering**™. It's about finding and fixing the "bugs" in our inner human software, and it is truly ground breaking work.

In this brilliant book, *Pure Awareness – Five Simple Techniques to Experience Your Essential Nature,* Tom has done something quite unique. He has distilled out of his vast experiences the simplest and most useful tools for creating profound and lasting change in your life. Even more importantly, he has identified exactly what to do to shift our old patterns of thoughts and feelings so that they no longer cause us to respond to life out of our old "knee jerk," conditioned responses. And if that weren't good enough, he has identified the essence of what we need to actually do in order to cultivate a whole new style of functioning that allows you to, as he says, "respond spontaneously to the needs of the moment with the fullness of your being." This is a potent combination and a whole new way of dismantling unwanted habits. It is unlike any other program for enriching your life that I've ever seen.

The unique thing about this book is that it is a practical guide that actually shows you how to really remove your inner barriers and conflicts. Lots of people have written about what you need to do to enjoy a better life; Tom actually gives you the tools for removing the things inside of you that keep tripping you up and getting in your way.

Recently I met with Tom and he showed me how to do the CORE Technique. Wow! I've done plenty of emotional release processing over the years but this was remarkably simple and especially deep and profound. I came out of something that had been nagging at me for weeks, and when it was complete, I felt a pervasive sense of bliss and expansion.

I am truly grateful to Tom for his help in my life and I am delighted that he is bringing his work out to share his insights and techniques to help others on a large scale. I know his desire is very similar to mine, to have a positive impact on the lives of many, many people. I know that through this book and Tom's pioneering work in creating **Human Software Engineering** he will accomplish this goal in a profound and powerful way.

Don't just read this book; actually do what it

recommends and you will find your life changing in ways that will inevitably lead you to have a quality of life experience that is beyond your wildest dreams.

Jack Canfield

Co-author, *Chicken Soup for the Soul*® series and *The Success Principles*™: *How to Get from Where You Are to Where You Want to Be.*

Appendix:
Additional Resources

CORE DYNAMICS COACHES

If you're having trouble getting started and feel like you need some guidance, feel free to contact us so that we can find a *Core Dynamics* coach for you. When you do speak to a *Core Dynamics* Coach, that person will take whatever time is needed to teach you to do the SEE Technique and the CORE Technique in a very specific and highly effective way. The coach will also help you to preempt anxious feelings that might try to come back by helping you to get in touch with the various situations that might trigger the anxiety. The *Core Dynamics* Coaches are available for single sessions or for a series of ongoing sessions for those who need them. Visit www.vaporizeyouranxiety.com/coaching to learn more about this valuable resource.

Core Dynamics Coaching is very different than traditional life coaching. We have a basic philosophy that great coaching comes from great people. And the way to access and live from your natural greatness that is already inside of you is to liberate it by vaporizing the emotional baggage that prevents your natural greatness from shining through.

Core Dynamics Coaches go through a rigorous training program that includes doing extensive work with the *Pure Awareness* Techniques to vaporize their own deepest emotional pain, fears, traumas and demons. They become experts on all the *Pure Awareness* Techniques and they receive training on some very advanced techniques not covered here. They come out the other side of this five-month training program as transformed individuals and highly effective coaches.

We have observed that the most important attribute of a really great coach is to have powerful coaching presence. This means that there are no internal or external distractions. *Core Dynamics* Coaches have a clean inner emotional landscape, and are as free of the 12 *Core Dynamics* of Human Conditioning as possible. We consider this to be the most important quality of *Core Dynamics* Coaches, and that quality must be demonstrated by the way they behave, by their coaching presence, and by the quality of their energy at the time they apply to become certified as a *Core Dynamics* Coach.

We are very careful to only certify people who exhibit a way of being that reflects this clear, powerful presence. Obviously they must have in-depth knowledge of each of

the *Core Dynamics*, understand the nature of the preverbal conditioning of each Core Dynamic, and be highly
proficient with the *Core Dynamics* Coaching protocol and
all of the *Pure Awareness* Techniques.

Great Life Technologies has certified hundreds of *Core
Dynamics* Coaches who can now help their clients vaporize
their anxiety and address a great range of other problems
in their lives. Clients of *Core Dynamics* coaches tend to
experience very rapid and profound breakthroughs that
conventional coaching can't achieve because it simply
doesn't have access to the necessary techniques. And the
breakthroughs happen so fast that sometimes several can
happen during a single coaching session! Whether or not
you have had any coaching in the past, you really owe
it to yourself to experience *Core Dynamics* Coaching, to
appreciate how powerfully distinct it is from other forms
of coaching. You'll be amazed at how different it is.

If you find that you can do the various techniques in
this book on your own, you may very likely still benefit
from working with a *Core Dynamics* Coach. In fact, your
familiarity with the techniques will allow you to dig
right in and easily begin work. The main advantage
of working with a *Core Dynamics* Coach is that instead
of waiting until your archived incomplete emotional
experiences are unexpectedly brought to the surface by
circumstances and events, you can take a pre-emptive
approach and proactively dig those old incompletions

out of your archives. Then you can vaporize them so that they won't prevent you from having the most magnificent life you can possibly have.

So whether you need help with vaporizing your anxiety or you'd like to get on the fast track to making sure that you've really done sufficient emotional house-cleaning to ensure that you don't have recurrences of anxiety in the future, visit us at www.vaporizeyouranxiety.com where you can find out how to get you connected with a *Core Dynamics* coach.

While you're there, check out the Great Life Programs like *Extraordinary Prosperity* or *Extraordinary Relationships.* These programs go into great depth in finding and vaporizing as much of the extensive conditioning that we all have around money and relationships. This is a unique and powerful way to transform these important aspects of your life.

OTHER BOOKS BY TOM STONE

The Power of How – Simple Techniques to Vaporize Your Ego and Your Pain-body

Pure Awareness—Five Simple Techniques for Experiencing Your Essential Nature

Be Smoke Free Now—Breakthrough Techniques for Becoming a Non-smoker Now and for the Rest of Your Life

These books are available on line at:

http://greatlifetechnologies.com/TStoneBooks.shtml

THE CORE DYNAMICS AUDIO CD SET

This is a set of audio CD's from a two-day seminar on the *Core Dynamics* of Common Problems given by Tom Stone. It can be ordered from the web at this address: greatlifetechnologies.com/CoreDynamicsCDSet.html (the URL is case sensitive)

CORE DYNAMICS COACH TRAINING

Would you like to become a certified *Core Dynamics* Coach? This is approximately a five-month program that begins with a four-day live seminar. It also includes learning the Core Competencies of coaching but from a *Core Dynamics* Perspective. *Core Dynamics* Coach Training is at: greatlifetechnologies.com/CDCTraining/Options. html

For other Books, Audio and Video Recordings, Products and Programs by Tom Stone please see http://greatlifetechnologies.com/catalog.html for more information.